Shatter Your Leadership Limits

*Better Results in Less Time with
Less Stress*

By

Bob Kantor

*Leadership Effectiveness Speaker,
Author, Coach and Consultant*

Preview Edition – June 2012

Early Praise for "Shatter Your Leadership Limits"

"Reading 'Shatter Your Leadership Limits - Better Results In Less Time With Less Stress' provides practical advice anyone can use to become a better leader. Bob Kantor brings his extensive years of leadership coaching experience to explain in 6 steps he calls "The Simple Leadership Life Cycle" invaluable guidance that will help you become an effective and respected team leader. A must read for anyone looking to move into a leadership role or anyone looking to sharpen their leadership capabilities."
- Joe Bruzzese, Senior IT Executive, Bloomberg, LP

"Whether you work in a large or small organization, this book will help you get right to the heart of leadership. Kantor, a superb executive coach, presents practical advice that actively assists managers in identifying opportunities for growth and fulfillment as leaders."
- Whitney Small, Regional Director of Communications, Ford Motor Company

"Great leaders are not Born – they are Built. Bob Kantor has taken stacks of management theory and years of leadership experience and developed a simple process that will help improve ANY leader, whether "wet behind the ears" or "long of tooth". If you will commit to "being" a better leader, the KEY to success of our complex organizations, and apply the practices presented in this book, you will emerge a better leader and more fulfilled as a person."
- Tim Rooney, President, PeopleMation

"The purpose of a good coach (whether for batting a pitched ball, singing like a diva, or inspiring good people for a desired outcome) is to help point out the simple things that we need to focus on to become better at what it is we are trying to improve. The secret to being a good coach is to understand the countless simple things that all need to come together on a consistent basis for improvement in the selected discipline.

In this book Bob is letting us in on his well-researched secrets about leadership, and then he is being the good coach who encourages us to practice, practice, practice. While you can't become a good leader from reading a book any more than you can from learning a secret handshake, you can become more aware of what you already know and how that can be applied to make you a better leader. Bob says, "Great leadership is simple." Fortunately, he backs that up with what it takes (some simple practices) to make it simple."
- *Carlos Recalde, Director of Enterprise Architecture, Barclays Capital*

"Kantor gets to the core of effective leadership by providing experience-based, practical, and straightforward techniques that will make it simpler for any manager to lead more effectively."
- *Mike Norton, VP & GM, Kerite Corporation*

"Kantor took years of leadership experience and developed a practical approach to becoming a more effective leader. Applying the practices outlined in this book will help any manager up her game."
- *Renee Furr, IT Director, Latrobe Specialty Steel*

"Shatter Your Leadership Limits delivers on its promise to help busy managers deliver better results in less time with less stress. Kantor's simple six point solution presents practical, proven tools and techniques - not only for overcoming the challenges inherent in leading others, but for thriving in the process. Field-tested over two years with over 100 professionals, Kantor's model for continual improvement will take your leadership to a new level."
- *James K. Papp, Corporate Executive and Author of Inquire Within: A Guide to Living in Spirit*

Printed in the United States of America.

First Printing: 2012

ISBN: 978-0-9859126-0-4

Dedication

To my two sons, for being wise beyond their years and sharing that wisdom with me every day.

And to my wife, for always accepting me as I am, and lovingly helping me understand what I can still become.

Acknowledgements

First, I would like to thank the many hundreds (thousands?) of professionals I have had the privilege to lead, coach, consult and work with over the past 20 years. Every one of you has taught me a great deal about the practice of leadership, and about who I am as a leader. There would be no content for this book without all of you and what you have shared with me over the years.

Second, and more specifically, I'd like to thank the hundred-plus people who over the past two years have helped me to focus those 20 years of experience into what has become the "Simple Leadership Life Cycle". With all your feedback on my questions, models, tools and techniques, I have been able to test and refine this material into a tool that has been proven valuable to a wonderfully diverse set of professionals. New and seasoned leaders, across a range of industries and functional domains, have helped me to clarify and simplify these ideas and practices that I've picked up during the course of my career.

Third, I want to thank my own Executive Coaches and Mentors, who over the years have helped me discover so much about leadership, about connecting with others, and about myself. Here I especially want to thank George Goldsmith of The Human Interface Group, Vince Rios of Rivers Consulting, Linda Miller of The Ken Blanchard Companies, Gregg Baron of Success-Sciences, Lisa Marshall of The Smart Work Company, Don Gardner of Gardner Project, and Tim Rooney of PeopleMation. Thank you each for your support, your probing questions, your skill and insight, and your complete commitment to holding me accountable for stepping up to my full potential.

Fourth, I need to recognize two gifted coaches and organizational change consultants, whose work became the foundation of my practices on Accountability and Communication.

Thanks to Gregg Baron and Jeff Grimshaw for teaching me the fundamentals that I've applied in so many situations, and with so many clients, over the years.

Fifth, my many thanks to Art Remnet of The Strategic Marketing Group, whose marketing coaching and advice, business process and technology design, web site development and management, and true friendship, have been instrumental in getting this effort to where it is.

Sixth, I'd like to thank Steve Harrison and his many talented coaches of the Quantum Leap program, who have guided me in how to take my knowledge and experience and turn it into two books, a radio show, articles in industry-leading publications, speaking engagements, and more. Shout outs here to Steve himself, and coaches Geoffrey Berwind, Raia King, Ann McIndoo, Brian Edmondson and Tamra Nashman.

Seventh, I wish to thank the senior editors and leaders at IDG Enterprise and their "CIO" publications and services, for seeing that we share a passion for enhancing the practice of IT management and leadership, and for helping me to amplify my voice. Thanks especially to Michael Friedenberg, President and CEO; Maryfran Johnson, Editor in Chief; Dan Muse, Executive Editor; and Monica Brunaccini, Director of Leadership Development.

Finally, and most importantly, my special thanks and deepest love, to my two very special sons and wonderful wife. They are the suns around which my universe revolves and the lights of my life. They give meaning to all that I do, and are my most valued coaches, trusted advisors, and dearest friends. They bring me hope and energy on cloudy days, and dance with me in the sunshine. I am here because of them...

Introduction

This book is written as a result of several experiences of the past few years, which motivated me to actually do what so many of us long to do, and actually write a book.

The first experience was the realization that I was covering several of the same topics over and over again in my coaching of IT leaders, and that there could be a natural progression through those topics much as there was with project life cycles and systems development life cycles. When so many of my clients expressed enthusiasm about the clarity that such an approach brought to their understanding and practice of leadership, I suspected there might be value in formalizing this approach.

The second experience was my visceral reaction to an editorial written by Maryfran Johnson and published in the May 1, 2011 issue of CIO Magazine. In it she wrote:

> "Despite the many metric tons of books and articles written about IT leadership, most of our workplaces are still better at identifying its absence than encouraging its growth.
>
> ...We just proved that again in our recent CIO Executive Council survey of 328 IT executives, which turned up a lamentable lack of leadership development activities at most companies today."

That simple observation, quantified with the startling clarity of the "survey of 328 IT executives..." hit me like a physical blow to the head. I realized that in order for my own behavior to remain congruent with my coaching practices, that I needed to move from observing the problem to taking constructive action to address it. That is, I had to step up and lead.

During this same time period I also shared the Simple Leadership Life Cycle with professionals in engineering, sales, marketing and product development. To my pleasant surprise, they all found it as helpful as did the IT professionals who first inspired its design. I came to realize that in today's all-the-time every-place digitally-interconnected business environment, that so many of our leaders had arrived in their roles because of their subject matter expertise, and not due to their demonstrated leadership skills.

That is, they'd not had the time that several generations of business leaders before them had, to learn the craft of leadership via a suitable period of apprenticeship to successful leaders. Instead, most of them (us...) had been thrust unceremoniously into their leadership roles with only a bit of classroom-based training, and the experience of getting ahead based upon their subject matter expertise.

This book is written for all such leaders. For all of you who have gotten to where you are based upon your subject matter mastery. That may be information technology, engineering, manufacturing, sales, marketing, science, or any other of the many knowledge specializations that drive business today.

I am writing this book with the hope that it may help you bridge the gap between what you know and believe about leadership, and what you actually do as a leader, day in and day out.

This book can be your guide to change a few of your leadership behaviors. If you are willing to actually change one or two of those behaviors, this book has the potential to enable you to deliver better results, in less time, and with less stress. And I truly hope you do...

Forward to the Preview Edition

If this book were a software application, it would be labeled Version 1.0. If it were a car, it would be the first year of a new model introduction.

As most of us know, initial releases of software and of cars often have bugs that still need to be ironed out, and improvements that need to be made. In the IT world, we call that process "testing in production."

That is indeed what this Preview Edition of "Shatter Your Leadership Limits" is. Even though it has now been through three complete rounds of editing at the hands of three talented professionals, it can still be better. It also could use a dozen or so diagrams and illustrations added to it, and could benefit from an appendix of tools and templates to make it easier to apply the many practices described within. Oh! And a workbook to move more people to action to apply the tools, and…

As many of us who have managed large projects have learned, every project could easily go on forever, as there are always opportunities to enhance the deliverable. And as we have also learned, at some point we need to claim success, declare the project completed, and then scope out another project to enhance the new product.

That's where we are today with Shatter Your Leadership Limits and this Preview Edition, in June of 2012. We're putting it in your hands now, and inviting you to apply it's ideas, practices, tools and techniques. We also invite you to send us your feedback. Please tell us what works for you and what doesn't work for you. Please point out our errors and missteps.

Thank you in advance for helping us to produce a better product with the next version.

Regards,
Bob Kantor
June 22, 2012

Contents

Chapter One
Why Leadership?
Or, "It's not enough to manage, we also need to inspire."

Let's begin with a story about a Corporate Executive. This story begins with, once upon a time, there was an Executive named Rosemary Roberts. Rosemary worked for a large company that was successfully capturing market share, expanding its services and products in the global marketplace, as well as growing its revenue.

As the company continued to expand, containing bottom-line expenses were an important part of the growth strategy which Rosemary worked hard to implement. One day, senior management asked Rosemary to develop more products and services. This was a tough task due to the increased size of the product and service base as well as the number of clients.

As a dedicated leader committed to excellence, she encouraged her team to work smarter and harder, alongside her. As hard as she worked, management kept demanding more products and services. Soon she and her team became overworked, and people began to get sloppy. Product quality began to decline. She knew, that unreliable product meant success problems in the market place.

She continued to inspire and motivate her team to work more hours, but people were less engaged, and burn out was starting to occur. To help the situation, she started work longer hours as well as weekends and as time went on, it became difficult to hire the caliber and quality of help needed. Stress kicked in. Overwhelm was the theme of the day.

One day there was huge error in the development and release of the product to the marketplace and the executive realize she was at the end of the runway. She didn't know how she could recover from the error and still maintain the momentum that was necessary for growth of the business while continuing at the current cost levels.

At that point, she realized that she needed some assistance. She needed to do something different if she was going to get different results. She remembered that the definition of insanity was continuing to do the same thing and expect different results. She realized that her practice of management had reached a point where it could legitimately qualify as insanity and that she owed it to herself, the people she worked with, and the company to do something different.

That's where the story ends for now.

Is there anything in that story that sounds familiar? Does that story, in fact, describe anything that you are dealing with in your work place today as a manager and a leader?

In reality, that story isn't about any one individual. However, after coaching over 100 executives over the past few years, that it is a story I hear over and over again in today's work environment. As businesses become global, and social networking and engaging our clients and the people in our marketplace become more important to how we deliver and develop products and services; we are all under more and more pressure to deliver more, deliver it faster, and with fewer resources.

All of my clients are striving for a series of simple steps

or a process to deliver more value in less time and with substantially reduced stress.

This book is about a series of simple techniques, that I call Leadership, that enable us to find more effective ways to leverage the people around us and the resources of our organization, not necessarily to do more, but to deliver more value which translates into doing more of the things that make a difference.

As we go through the tools and techniques in each chapter, we will look at:

- How to prioritize;

- How to manage time and energy;

- How to delegate;

- How to hold people accountable and create conditions of accountability;

- How to significantly improve the effectiveness of performance management and professional development efforts; and

- How to communicate more effectively.

All of these help us to better leverage the people with whom we work and enable us to show up as more effective leaders.

Here's another story, about Dr. Martin Luther King Jr., one of the great leaders of our time, and that iconic speech where he stood on the steps of the Lincoln Memorial. Imagine this fictitious version of the story. As he looked out upon the crowd of hundreds of thousands of people he proclaimed, "I have a dream." And then he paused, put his hand to his chin, looked up at the sky and said, "But, you know, I'm not really sure that we're up for it." What impact would *that* version of the story have had on the movement to end segregation?

As leaders, that's the challenge we have every day. We face significant odds trying to live our vision and strategic intention for our organizations, and we find ourselves wondering, as leaders, "Are we up for it? Are our teams up for it? Are our organizations up for it?"

There are some very simple approaches to leadership that we can employ and apply to overcome any doubts we may have, and effectively enable our team to achieve what we are dreaming about and striving to achieve.

Many of us do this every day. Such leadership doesn't just reside within the business world. It is all around us—in our classrooms where great teachers, against all odds, inspire and move children to tremendous achievements.

We see it on the stage in a symphony orchestra where a conductor, who likely is not an expert player of any of the instruments, can enable and inspire the musicians to produce beautiful music.

Think about sitting in front of a child, or with one of your children, and reading them a story. Relish for a moment the look in that child's eyes when he or she gazes up with love and affection.

Think about sitting around the dining table as a family, talking about the day and giving each member of the family an opportunity to share whatever is on their mind, in an environment of mutual trust and respect.

These are all examples of leadership. Some of these are situations that many of us find ourselves in from day-to-day.

I am frequently asked in my leadership coaching practice, whether everyone can be a leader. Based upon experience, it is my belief that we are all born as leaders and have the potential to be great leaders. For those of us that aren't already there, all that we're lacking is a simple model, a simple plan to implement that model, and simple tools and techniques to execute that plan.

We will be putting together that model, sharing a very simple plan, and going through six relatively simple techniques with tools to better enable anyone to be a more effective leader.

Great leadership is simple. It does not require complex knowledge. It's less about how much we know and more about what we do with what we know. A little bit of guidance will enable everyone to be more effective leaders.

Why is this so important today? One of the challenges is the complexity of the world within which we live and operate. Whether it's business, the arts, education, or the social communities within which we participate, complexity precludes our ability to be both a subject matter expert or practitioner, and a leader. There is just too much information out there today.

The day of the manager as the most technically knowledgeable individual in a team or group, is over. This makes the process of leadership a very important skill for the achievement of any outcome that we strive for in any realm.

It's been my experience that as any one of us becomes a more effective leader, we enable and inspire the people with whom we work to also be better leaders, and thereby create organizational leverage.

I'm often asked about how applicable some of the more

fundamental concepts are that we cover in my leadership coaching programs, given how much change is occurring in the world today.

I respond that to some degree our brains are fairly hardwired. And while we have evolved over time, the changes to our brains have evolved over thousands of years or even hundreds of thousands of years, and that that this material reflects our neural hardwiring. And to the extent that over the last 200 years, the evolution of our brains has really not been significant, these timeless principles and practices still apply.

And, as I've learned from the people with whom I've worked over the last several years, these principles and practices apply in just about any environment where groups of people strive to work together.

Let's take a look at one such example of the way we are wired, and its implications for the importance of leadership and our approach to leadership.

Very often I hear from my clients, that as leaders, one of their challenges is that people resist change. I ask them whether there may be the possibility that people actually don't resist change, but in fact, resist being changed.

If you reflect on that for just a bit, you may realize that this amounts to the difference between telling people what needs to be done and how to do it, versus inviting them or inspiring them to figure out what needs to be done or how to do it.

A couple of years ago one of my clients came up with the idea that good leadership is less about instructing people about what to do and how to do it, and instead is about inspiring people to do things that serve them in terms of their growth and development as individuals, while at the same time adding significant value to the organizations of which they are a part.

To give us a little more experience with the idea of change and resistance to change, I'd like to invite you to join me in a very simple exercise.

If you would, take your two hands, hold them out in front of you, and clasp your fingers such that one thumb is resting upon the other thumb. Make a note of which thumb is on top. Is it the left or right thumb?

Now, unclasp your hands. Again, hold your hands in from of you. This time clasp your hands together and put the other thumb on top. Take a moment and experience how that feels. If you are like most people, you will be experiencing mild discomfort. Though, some people experience quite significant or severe discomfort. And a very few people don't experience any discomfort at all. But the reality is that most of us not only notice the difference, but are uncomfortable with the difference.

So, what does this prove? What does it illustrate?

We've just subjected ourselves to a ridiculously trivial behavior change. And the behavior change was putting the other thumb on top when we clasp our hands. And yet, most of us notice discomfort, if not outright resistance to making that change.

So, what do we learn from that? Well, first off, we have the experience that even trivial change, shouldn't be treated as a trivial exercise. In fact, we can also infer that in order to make any kind of change, given the fact that we need to overcome discomfort for even small changes, there must be a compelling reason to make the change.

And that reason needs to be compelling for each and every one of us who wants to make a change. And, we need to be constantly aware of that compelling reason. We also need to be able to address a series of issues and challenges so that as we strive to sustain or maintain the change, we can overcome those issues and challenges.

If you've ever watched an expert working a process, like a basketball player running down the court and making behind the back passes, or an artisan woodworker turning a table leg on a wood lathe, or a leader standing in front of a room inspiring members of an organization to take action — what you're observing is an expert making the hard plays look much easier than they are.

These experts apply their knowledge and experience, and they do actually work more easily than others. That requires significant practice and learning, as well. With the simple techniques that we will work through, as well as some practice, you too will be able to work more easily in difficult leadership situations.

Great leadership is much more about taking action than it is about having big thoughts. Philosophy is about having great thoughts, and a person with great thoughts is usually thought to be a very smart person. A person with great action is often a very strong leader. Leadership, then, is application of the knowledge we have via a strong set of skills.

We will not attempt to teach you about leadership. That's something you can learn in a classroom, and you probably already have all of the knowledge that you need. We will be help you bridge the gap between what you know about leadership and what you do on a regular basis as a leader.

We will encourage you to practice a very simple set of

techniques, so you can effectively apply what you know. It's not what you know nearly as much as putting what you know into action, distinguishing what works and what doesn't work, making small improvements along the way and continuing to learn and grow.

One of the other challenges that I've observed over many years of coaching and helping leaders develop their skills, is that many of us pursue the practice of leadership without a clear plan of action. Our desired outcomes are often not clear enough, i.e., the "what" of what we're trying to accomplish is not explicit in our minds. Our conditions of satisfaction, the measures of success, aren't well articulated. The tools and processes that we can use (the "how") aren't identified, or the schedule and frequency (the "when") of applying these tools and processes is not clear.

Imagine a project like releasing a new product, developing new services, moving a warehouse or renovating an office facility. Would you attempt to do that without a clearly articulated project plan?

Good leaders wouldn't undertake such an effort without a good plan. And yet, when it comes to leadership, we often approach our leadership without a plan. We need a plan for the development and execution of our leadership practices. We need to include milestones for success and dates against which we can track our progress and measure our success. Unfortunately, that's something very few of us do. We need to have a simple model or structure for how these practices fit together and deliver the result that we want. This book is a template for such a plan. We'll provide more detail in Chapter Ten, which is about moving into action.

You will identify a series of topics or practices that you

want to either develop or improve upon for your leadership. And then, for each quarter in the next 12 months, you will identify either some actions that you want to take or some targets that will demonstrate that you have achieved your objective.

We will put into place a periodic review process so that you can measure your progress and success, or lack of progress and success, in such a way that you will have plenty of time to take corrective action, so that one way or another, you will achieve or improve your leadership skills.

I have been teaching, coaching and helping develop leaders in business organizations for over 20 years. Over 20 years ago I had an opportunity to focus on leadership development and coaching part-time as I was growing and becoming a leader. After 20 years, I had the opportunity to focus on leadership development and coaching full-time with the start of my own coaching and consulting business.

In the process of coaching over 100 leaders full-time in the past several years, I've had the opportunity to distill business leadership into a handful of simple practices that anyone can learn, and that most people can easily and quickly put into practice.

I call these Practices for a good reason. There may be no idea in the following material that you have not heard before, but knowing this information is not the same as practicing it day in and day out. The regular practice of these simple ideas is what makes us good and strong leaders. It is also the practice that enables us to do the same simple things very well, much like an expert. Though these things are simple, they are not easy and they require regular practice in order to do them effectively, and in difficult and challenging situations.

Over the course of seven chapters, we will go through a series of six leadership Practices. We will look at examples of where they have worked and where they haven't worked. We will look at some simple processes that you can apply in your own leadership practice, so that you will become a much stronger and more confident leader and deliver higher value results. You will do so in less time and you will do so with significantly less stress.

Thank you for joining me.

Chapter Two
The Simple Leadership Life Cycle
Or, "It's not enough to be committed, we also need a proven strategy."

Recently, I was working with a relatively new manager in my leadership coaching program. He had been in his management role for only eight months and though he was working hard, he was having difficulty transitioning from an individual contributor to a team leader. After several exploratory conversations, we discovered that his major problem was that he didn't have a plan or a structure for how to proactively and consistently apply his leadership skills.

That was a common theme for many clients with whom I'd been working that were new to leadership. In an effort to provide structure and to them to give them a jumpstart, I created and defined what I've since called the Simple Leadership Life Cycle.

This Simple Leadership Life Cycle is defined by its six soft skills. These are the leadership capabilities that are necessary for leaders to effectively engage each other, their colleagues, and members of their teams.

This set of soft skills is a repeating cycle that reflects the first challenge many leaders face. Because of their lack of a simple plan with which to apply their skills, they are unable to achieve consistent results. Their leadership activities are ad hoc and simply a reaction to situations as they occur.

We have found that by challenging them to lead in a more

proactive manner, and by routinely and continuously running through this cycle, their personal leadership impact improves dramatically.

We have seen over and over again that when we undertake a project without a plan, or with an insufficient plan, we are much less likely to achieve our results in the time frame and with the level of quality to which we aspire.

We find that the better our plan is, the more proactively we can anticipate, identify and address challenges before they have a negative impact on our project. And overall, everyone involved in the project feels better about the way the project is progressing and finds it to be a rewarding situation within which to work.

The Simple Leadership Life Cycle is like creating or applying a project plan to the project that we call leadership, which in effect, is leading a function or a group of people.

The Simple Leadership Life Cycle has six soft skills as follows:
- Strategic Intent,
- Prioritization,
- Delegation,
- Accountability,
- Performance Management, and
- Communication.

Because this is a leadership cycle, we don't end with a full stop, and we begin the cycle again. Having communicated and achieved a particular result, we take another look at our Strategic Intent, adjust our Prioritization, continue with Delegation, apply Accountability or create new Accountability situations, continue to hold Performance Management conversations, Communicate again, and reassess Strategic Intent.

The Simple Leadership Life Cycle does not always occur in a complete sequence, going through the entire cycle in totality. Instead, we apply the Simple Leadership Life Cycle many times, in parallel, during the course of the day or week. For every leadership initiative that we are pursuing, we may be at a different point in the leadership cycle. And not every situation requires every step of the cycle.

For a particular project, we may be in the Delegation phase of that project. For a process improvement or an operational issue that we are resolving, we may be in the Performance Management phase of the cycle. When we are doing annual business planning, we may be pursuing the process of annual business planning at the Prioritization phase of the process. And then a couple of weeks or months later, we will have moved completely through the Leadership Cycle and will be ready to begin again with Strategic Intent.

We will provide a detailed description of the tools and techniques that we teach our clients. Below is a quick summary of the key leverage that our clients realize as they improve their capabilities with each of these skills.

Strategic Intent

This is similar to clarifying the Strategic Intent of a company or a corporate department. In the Simple Leadership Life Cycle it is applied to each individual's role as a leader. For example, many leaders enter into conversations and meetings with a tactical intent to obtain a specific decision or to drive a specific task to completion. When they instead strategically set their intent to enhance their relationships with participants and/

or to build a more shared understanding; their approach is usually more effective than more typical direct frontal attacks.

Prioritization

This applies to each leader's focus for their day, week, or month. We are often asked to help our clients with what they identify initially as a time management problem. Instead, we address this as an insufficient Prioritization of their attention. We help them create clarity around what is truly important for them to achieve. This Prioritization then begins to help them resolve their time management challenges.

Having addressed Prioritization, we then have them use a forced ranking process to create actionable priorities and to allocate specific blocks of time to those priorities. Later we'll detail that process and the tools that people often use for execution.

Delegation

In order for leaders to have the necessary time and attention to fully engage their colleagues across their companies, and to focus their attention on their true priorities, they often need to significantly increase the amount of work that they Delegate. This can usually be done more quickly, more completely, and more effectively than most of us believe when they are supported by the skills below.

Accountability

We all want every member of our organizations to deliver results and take ownership for overcoming obstacles. There's a simple formula for creating Accountability or Conditions of

Accountability.

It was defined years ago by our colleagues Grimshaw and Baron. The secret they identified is to communicate clear and credible expectations, create compelling positive and negative consequences, and then to lead ongoing conversations that are grounded in facts and evidence. When our staff members are Accountable, increasing Delegation is much more viable.

Performance Management

Applying all of these skills creates an environment of high Performance. And, applying these skills each day, with everyone with whom we interact, is our definition of Performance Management. That is, it's a continuous process of team member engagement, and not just a periodic conversation about performance. What many leaders often identify as "difficult conversations" become relatively easy and routine when they apply the Simple Leadership Life Cycle over and over and over again.

Communication

Here, we define Communication as much more than the message we give or send to people. This skill is about the influence we have and the outcomes we generate. We identify a key missing component in most leaders' communication process, which is to leverage their target audience's beliefs.

We demonstrate in our coaching practice that by working backwards from the outcome we want to generate, to the beliefs that our audiences hold and need to change in order to take the action we desire, we are then in a much better position to identify the information and the delivery mechanism that we need to achieve our desired outcome.

This then leads us back to Strategic Intent, which is informed and adjusted with each reiteration of the Simple Leadership Life Cycle.

The business leaders to whom we teach this Cycle, and related components, experience much higher levels of employee and organizational engagement, which enables them to deliver better results in less time and with less stress.

How to Get Value from This Book

There are thousands of good books on leadership and many of us have attended useful and valuable leadership classes and training programs, as well. It is my desire and hope that this will not be just another one of the many books that you read and then put on your shelf, or one of the many processes or programs that you go through, enjoy, see value in and then don't apply. That's really the crux of the matter. Application of this material is how you're going to gain value for your time and effort.

In my coaching practice, most of the people I work with tell me, and report on anonymous surveys, that they realized a tremendous amount of value from the work we did together. They go on to identify ways in which they are working or behaving more effectively as leaders, and delivering higher value results to their companies or organizations. As we come to the close of the coaching program, 15% to 20% of the participants observe and share that the leadership coaching program has changed their lives.

The difference between the people who believe that their

lives have been changed, and everyone else who simply derive value and benefit from the program, is the degree to which the individuals have suspended their discomfort around change, and have implemented the new practices and processes learned in the coaching program.

We have all experienced that when we try something new and change our behavior, like changing our diets, beginning an exercise program, or changing our golf swing, we experience a certain degree of discomfort.

Those of us who successfully integrate the new behavior from a trial into a habit are the ones who can push through and work through the discomfort until we have truly internalized the new behavior.

Most of us, when we experience discomfort, modify our behaviors to eliminate the source of the discomfort. In the case of trying a new leadership behavior, we experience discomfort. Our immediate and automatic reaction is to eliminate the source of the discomfort, which is the new leadership behavior that we learned and decided to implement. And that's why so many of us find it difficult to implement new behaviors, whether they're leadership behaviors or lifestyle changes.

Regardless of the book or program you go through, for any kind of professional or lifestyle change you desire to make, the real value that you can and will experience only occurs when you consistently apply the change in your behavior.

There are many research studies on how long it takes before you can work through discomfort and habitualize a new behavior. For some of us, and for select behaviors, it can be relatively quick and simple. It might be only a couple of days, or a few weeks. For other changes, it requires more time.

One of my favorite studies on the subject was done at NASA with astronauts who were in training to spend time on the space shuttle. The astronauts wore glasses with prisms that inverted their visual field, so that everything appeared upside down.

NASA anticipated that over time the astronauts would learn to accommodate the inverted images and would recalibrate all of their movements and functions, much like a dentist learns to work with the image reversed in a mirror.

The experiment progressed, and after 27-31 days, each and every one of the astronauts had the very same, but very unexpected, experience. Within that five-day window, every astronaut's visual field suddenly flipped. What had been an upside down image was no longer perceived by the brain as inverted. They didn't have to accommodate the inverted visual field anymore, because the brain had basically reprogrammed or, if you will, rewired itself, so that the nerve impulses coming through the optic nerve were being perceived and processed as if the image had not been inverted by the prismatic glasses.

Using that as one of our data points, we can infer that significant behavioral changes take somewhere around 30 days to fully integrate into and through our nervous systems.

I invite you to seriously consider pushing through whatever discomfort you may have as you experiment with the six behaviors or tools and techniques in the Simple Leadership Life Cycle. Give yourself at least 30 days of working with these new techniques, tools and behaviors, to fully integrate them. Hopefully you will realize the extensive benefits that we know they can provide, because of the hundreds of people who have been through this program and have successfully applied these simple techniques.

I can almost guarantee that if you will give a solid 30 days of effort, you have the potential to change your life as a leader. Join us as we continue on to drill down into much more detail into each one of these components of the Leadership Cycle, in terms of how to execute them and the tools that we can use to effectively leverage them.

Let's move ahead and dive into the first of the Simple Leadership Life Cycle techniques, Managing Our Strategic Intent.

Chapter Three
Managing Strategic Intent
Or, "It's not enough to be right, we also need to be helpful."

Over the last several years many of our coaching clients have shared how often the six techniques in the Simple Leadership Life Cycle, translated into enabling them to be more effective leaders at home. They improved relationships with their spouses and their children. They were especially grateful because these techniques also helped them improve relationships with their teenagers.

Leadership does not necessarily only enable us to realize more of what we want to achieve in a business environment. Leadership is a set of core skills that enable us to be more effective in all aspects of our lives; we can be more effective leaders in the workplace, and at home with our families. And, we can also be more effective leaders in our communities, religious groups, and associations in which we participate.

The six simple techniques that we will be exploring together and learning how to improve, have the potential to change our lives. In today's world, leadership for many of us is a core competency.

When my children were young, we used to go to the Bronx Zoo on a fairly frequent basis, and on each trip we would see a different section of the zoo. One day, we decided to go see the elephants, and as we walked over, we saw that the elephant house was under construction. We saw lots of earth moving machines, big backhoes, bulldozers and dump trucks, in the process of knocking down the old elephant house as they began digging the foundation for the new one.

As we kept trying to pull our eldest son over to the side of the compound, where the elephants were hanging out and doing elephant-like things, he kept pulling us back to the earth moving machines. He wanted to watch the earth moving machines rebuild the habitat, which he found to be much more interesting than the elephants themselves.

We resisted his desire for a while, and then remembered the reason we had come to the zoo was because of our intention to spend quality time with our young son. The animal versus machine choice wasn't central to that intention. And, in fact, the opportunity that he was presenting to us was to fully realize our intention of spending quality time together on a beautiful afternoon, by watching the construction equipment being operated and rebuilding the habitat. Watching the elephants really was immaterial, once we were clear on our intention to spend quality time together.

This story introduces the idea that, in order to be effective leaders, first and foremost, we need to be clear on our intent.

This next story, from the business environment, is more current. One of my coaching clients is an executive director for a global automobile company, and she works in the Asia-Pacific region. She has a line management role, in a fairly large organization with a broad range of roles and span of control.

We had been talking about her roles and responsibilities, and one afternoon she said that more and more frequently she found herself helping to change the culture in the organization. The term she used to summarize the change that she was striving to support was "new company versus old company." In the interest of honoring confidentiality, I will not use any specifics beyond that level of detail.

While her line responsibility was not in managing the culture change itself, she realized how essential and central that culture change was to the day-to-day line operating objectives that she and her organization wished to manifest. From time to time, the old company would rear its head and try to impinge on some of the initiatives or types of changes being addressed by the new company. When this happened, she saw it as an opportunity, and would get involved and work through those cultural change issues to reinforce and support the growth and habitualization of the new company values and procedures.

This is another example of being clear when managing of our intentions, and can be referred to as managing our strategic intent. Because she saw and grasped the strategic issues, she saw the opportunity and chose to rise above the day-to-day operational challenges as those situations presented themselves. And it was that clarity around her strategic intent that enabled her to:

1. Identify the situation;
2. Rise to the occasion; and
3. Effectively address the opportunity.

That became a very significant component of her leadership role, of her presence in the company, and to her contribution of value.

First and foremost, great leaders don't worry about managing their time or improving their communications. They focus on their intentions and their energy. They know that if their intentions are appropriate and if they apply their energy to achieve those intentions, the rest tends to take care of itself.

I don't mean to imply that managing one's time and communications is immaterial. There is a very specific reason that the Simple Leadership Life Cycle begins with strategic intent and then moves into the other areas. And as we discussed earlier, the Simple Leadership Life Cycle is a continuous cycle. Represented as a circle, it doesn't necessarily have a beginning and an end.

In each new initiative, incident or transaction, to the degree that we can be clear and set our strategic intent, for ourselves, and perhaps also for those around us, we stand a much better chance of successfully achieving our desired outcome.

As we clarify and set our intentions, we can state them implicitly for our own clarity and benefit, or we can go beyond internal clarification and explicitly share them, as a way to increase engagement with those around us.

Very often as we explore with our clients the changes they are going to make, we invite them to consider the possibility of discussing the changes that they are implementing when they go back into their work organizations. As we change and show up differently within and in front of the people we lead and work with, they will ask themselves these questions:

- Why is she/he doing this?
- Why is she/he doing this differently?
- What is behind the change that I am observing and experiencing?

Often people will observe, "He's changing the way he does things because he thinks this is going to work better," or "She's changing because she must have read a book or been through a class."

Our coaching experience is that when we make our intentions explicit, we stand a much better chance of raising the level of engagement and collaboration with the people around us:

1. They don't have to wonder; they know why things are changing.

2. We have the opportunity to share the rationale that we have used in deciding to make the change, which significantly empowers us in making the new behavior, and encourages them in joining us or collaborating with us in leveraging the new behavior.

An example may be changing the way we create conditions of accountability, about which we will go into more detail in Chapter Six.

Sometimes, when we put more structure around how we delegate and hold people accountable, it can be perceived and experienced as too much management, often labeled "micromanagement". By getting very clear about intending to provide more support, everyone can be more successful. Clarity of intent goes a long way to ensure that we can realize the results we expect from the changes we're making.

That decision of whether to set our intentions implicitly for ourselves, or explicitly with and for everyone around us, has an impact on company culture. The reality is that we don't create culture. Culture is something that occurs as a byproduct of our behavior. To the extent that our behavior is more consistent, we create a stronger culture. The opposite is also true. To the degree that our behavior is less consistent, we create a weaker culture. We can have behavior that creates a consistently bad culture, or we can have a set of consistent behaviors that create a better and more constructive culture.

The way we and our colleagues behave defines our culture. Unfortunately, there are no shortcuts or tricks to creating a culture. As leaders, it reflects who we are and how we are, day in and day out.

Part of setting intention is to give some thought to what it is we're trying to accomplish with each of our interactions. In today's world, with its increased complexity and high degree of network interaction in and out of the workplace, it is no longer enough to be right. We also have to be helpful.

This is most often a challenge in organizations where technical competency leads to leadership enhancement and rising through the ranks. This frequently happens with technology professionals in the financial services industry, engineers in the manufacturing industry, and scientists in the pharmaceutical industry.

In each of those domains, very often the people who become managers and senior leaders are people who were very strong and successful based upon their technical competency. And as they rose through the ranks, they found themselves spending less time exercising that technical knowledge, and more time exercising their leadership competencies. When they were individual contributors, often their success was based on being able to come up with a "right answer" and then persuading others about the correctness of their answer or solution. As their role shifts to leadership, it becomes more important to build consensus and to inspire others to take effective, consistent and aligned action. The ability to convince people, with different perspectives and viewpoints, of a single correct or right answer becomes greatly diminished.

Some of my favorite examples for this simple truism occur in the personal realm. Think of a situation where you know somebody who has recently quit smoking or is trying to quit smoking. You're sitting with them and as they're fumbling to light up a cigarette, you look at them and say, "Are you sure you really want to do that?"

Another example would be a loved one on a diet who is seeking to lose weight. After the dinner dishes are cleared, they open the cupboard and pull out a box or a bag of cookies. As they're opening the container, you say to them, "Are you sure you really want to have a cookie now?"

In both of those cases, you're probably right. Based on their goals and objectives, it's a very valid question to ask. And yet, is your approach going to be perceived as helpful, or is it going to create frustration? Might either of the individuals in those two situations be more motivated to either light up a cigarette or eat a cookie as a way to resist being manipulated in a very uncomfortable situation?

I see a great deal of this in the professional and business world, particularly among the scientific or expert domains, where people get hung up on being right. Then the argument over what is right obscures the greater goal of what is useful and what will work. So, very often in the coaching process, we will invite people, as they consider how to pursue a challenge or a problem, to ask themselves these questions:

- How could I approach this in a way that the largest number of people would see it as helpful?
- How can I constructively challenge and facilitate

what is going on?

- How can I enhance what is going on by being helpful, rather than by focusing on what is right?

That leads us to another perspective on setting our intention. It is our belief that a fundamental intention of each one of our interactions is to enhance our relationships, regardless of the detail of the transactions themselves. We would even submit that when we are a leader, the primary purpose of every interaction is to enhance our relationships. Many of us have experienced, that when we have strong relationships, we can have more open and honest communication, we can deal with challenges effectively and quickly, and we have fewer breakdowns.

Often when we work with new leaders or junior managers, they come to us with problems, perhaps having to deal with a performance issue around quality or timeliness with one of their staff members. We ask them what their intention is when they have that performance management conversation. More often than not, we hear answers like, "To get them to stop making mistakes," or "To get them to deliver things faster," or "To get them to show up for work on time."

What we then ask them is that they consider whether that is the primary objective, or whether that's the secondary objective, and we give them the following scenario.

> If your intention is simply to have that individual change their behavior, you will approach the conversation in a very specific way, and your behavior will be experienced in a very specific way. Instead, imagine that you approach the same situation with a primary intention to deepen your relationship with that member of

your team. If, as you sit down to talk about what's going on with the quality of their work, you are very aware of wanting to enhance your relationship with that individual, how might your demeanor be different? How might your tone be different? How would your language be different? How would your energy level be different?

It doesn't take very much reflection to recognize that by choosing a different intention, the entire approach will be different. One intention is much more likely to be successful than the other.

Here is another tool that we frequently explore for applying different intentions in one of two ways. In the coaching process, we often explore using questions versus statements as a way to interact, engage, and express our intentions. This comes down to a lot of neuroscience around how our brains are wired. The reality is that over the last couple of hundred years, there hasn't been a significant evolutionary change in this level of our anatomy.

The impact of using questions versus statements has probably been the same for the last couple of hundred years, and will probably be the same for the rest of our lifetimes and more.

All of the evidence from the studies on using questions vs. statements, points to a fact that when people make statements directed at us, or when we hear statements, we immediately have at least some level of resistance. And when people ask us questions, we very often feel and become much more engaged. In fact, there are salespeople who use that well-documented data point and use questions in a manipulative fashion. Unfortunately, we find it difficult to resist manipulative behavior when the behavior is shrouded in a question format.

For example, far too often I experience dinner hour telephone calls from fundraisers who start with, "Do you care about the fact that 25% of the children in the United States go to bed hungry each night?" When asked a question like that, it's very difficult for us not to engage. Of course I care, and it's almost automatic for me to answer the question with, "Well, yes, I care."

And then something clicks in my brain that says: "Wait a minute, it's my dinnertime. This is a fundraising telephone call that is intruding on my private time. This may or may not be a viable and bona fide charitable organization, and I'm being manipulated." I very quickly recognize that I'm being manipulated and choose not to participate further.

Having said that and digressed, let's come back to the idea of using questions versus statements as leaders.

When we engage people around us by asking questions, whether they are a member of our team, a peer across the organization, or more senior level people, we immediately heighten the level of engagement in those interactions. And if we ask helpful and very useful questions, we can very often move conversations and problem solving sessions along much more quickly than if we walk in, make statements, and try to demonstrate that we are right.

In the process of asking questions, people will very often open up and examine their own assumptions. They will be more likely to listen to us and to others who are asking questions. Whereas when we use statements, people tend to dig in their heels, become entrenched, and get focused on how to have the right versus wrong conversation.

If this is not something that feels intuitively right to you, I invite you to do your own experiment. Pick a relatively simple situation where a consensus needs to be built, have a conversation with one individual and approach it with a series of statements to see if you can convince them of your position. And then in a similar situation, use a series of questions to walk them through your thought process hoping to have them realize the same outcome on their own, as a result of thinking through the questions as you thought them through. Then compare the two experiences.

There is another type of leadership challenges where setting our intent pays big dividends. That is the situation where we believe we need to say "No" to requests or situations, and still want to be seen as team players. We hear this problem over and over, where individuals try to stand up for what they believe is in the organization's best interest by resisting certain pat solutions, hasty solutions or approaches, and want to take a more strategic approach. And more often than not, when they say, "Wait a minute, we think that's a mistake," or "We think there's a better way," they get labeled as not being team players. Sound familiar?

Here is a powerful technique that I and many of my clients have used over the years. This is not my invention. The opportunity here is not necessarily to learn something entirely new, but to apply what we are learning in new and different ways. I'd like to share with you a model titled, *The Power of a Positive No*. To give credit where credit is due, this came out of the Harvard Negotiation program. Twenty years ago William Ury broke onto the *New York Times* bestseller list with a book called *Getting To Yes*. His fourth book, *The Power of a Positive No*, is the other side of the same coin.

This is an approach to leverage positive intentions to say *"No"* to a specific request or situation, while saying *"Yes"* to enhancing the relationship and supporting the strategic intention of the organization. This is a very simple three-step process that I'll oversimplify here.

When we are asked to do something or support something that we do not think is strategically appropriate, we start by saying yes to shared values. If someone comes to us and says, "Could you please make these changes to this information system?"

And as we're listening to them we're saying to ourselves, *"Yes, we could do that but in the process of doing that, we would actually be creating a situation in the future that would make it much more cumbersome and costly to grow and enhance this application, as we know we will need to do as the business evolves."*

As we listen to the request, we might respond by articulating our shared values:

> "Based upon the fact that we all believe that the business is growing rapidly and our systems will have to evolve rapidly as the business changes; based upon our shared belief that we are trying to serve the broadest number of users out in the business world as possible, rather than any select subset; based upon our shared belief that we want to be making the smallest possible changes for the largest possible impact; this is a request that we would actually recommend that we together say no to, because it will..."

Then go through the reasons that this request would be inconsistent with the shared values that you just summarized.

The third step in the process is to offer an alternative.

> "While that particular request doesn't appear to be consistent with our shared values, we can think of one or two other approaches that would be. Can you give me just a couple of minutes to outline them for you?"

Or in a situation where you don't have a ready or pat answer, the request might be something more along these lines:

> "Can you give me a couple of days to confer with the rest of the team to come up with an approach that would be more consistent with the values that we hold in common?"

The result or experience that the requester has is that:

1. We were aligned in terms of the values that we both share and hold as important, which is a "*Yes*" experience.

2. It is true that they got a "*No*", in terms of their specific request of the moment, but it was in the context of a larger "*Yes*".

3. Rather than leave it as a, "*No*, we're not going to do that; go away, don't bother me," there was a "*Yes*" to coming up with a more effective and higher value solution.

Let's now tackle a couple of additional ways to approach setting or clarifying our intent. Often in our coaching work, as people begin to identify a problem, they use language along the lines of, "I have to." We frequently ask them, after they have explained the problem, whether there is an option to reframe "I have to" into "I choose to." This relates to our earlier assertions around the use of questions versus statements, and has to do with how our brains are wired. ("I have to" implies we are faced with a statement. "I choose to" implies we were faced with a question that allowed us a choice of response.)

When we feel or believe that we have to do something, we trigger our fight or flight response, which involves resistance. Even though we may believe we need to do something, as we think through, "I have to," we automatically set up our own resistance. If we were to say to someone else, "Because of the firm's policies, you have to...," we are also setting up their resistive wiring and responses.

On the other hand, if we use the framing of choosing to do things, that usually brings us closer to being happy, or a desired end state or feeling of well-being. For example, "I have to skip dessert because I'm trying to lose weight," doesn't leave us feeling very good. "I choose to skip dessert because I'm improving my health and reducing my weight," is a much more positive response. It leaves us feeling stronger, in control, and empowers us to be more successful in sticking with the healthy behavior.

Let's look at that in the workplace:
- "I have to show up at work at 6:30 in the morning because I was told to," versus "I choose to be at work at 6:30 in the morning, because that enables me to be more effective, given the nature of the work that I need to get done."
- "I have to change my behavior if I am going to be a more effective leader," versus "I choose to change my leadership behaviors, so I can be a

more effective leader."

Think of a couple of your own situations where you felt that you had to do something, and then reframe it as your choice to do it. You can directly experience the visceral difference between those two approaches.

Here is another angle on setting our intention. How many times have you asked someone a question and received the response, "I don't know"? How many times have you yourself been challenged to deal with a problem or a situation and immediately thought or stated, "I don't know"?

One of the most common obstacles that we see in successful leadership development is the phrase, "I don't know." Many of our clients ask, "What do I do when I'm trying to help someone change what they're doing by using questions to invite them to consider alternatives, and they say, "I don't know"?

This often happens in team meetings when staff doesn't engage in problem solving, don't offer ideas, and say they "don't know." When I ask my coaching clients for other approaches they might try to better engage their staff, they too respond with, "I don't know."

I was working with an entrepreneur client who provides business services to large global companies, and who was struggling with a specific business development challenge. And after my repeated questions about his approach, he finally said, "I don't know, I just don't know."

Can you recall the last time someone asked you a question and you replied, "I don't know"? Take a moment to think about it. What was the situation? What were you thinking about right after you said those three words? Take a minute and please recall such a situation before continuing.

My experience is that the single biggest reason that "I don't know" is an obstacle for so many of us, is because when we hear it or think it, we consider it a final conclusion. We take it to mean that we are stuck, have no way to move forward, and are at the end of the line of our ability to figure out where to go next or how to move on.

What would happen if the next time you uttered or heard those words, you thought instead, "Okay, so how do I figure that out?" What if "I don't know" were simply an acknowledgment that at that very moment in time, you didn't have a ready answer? Would that free you up to move on and continue to search for ideas, solutions and next steps?

My clients almost always come up with useful ideas following the moment they realize that "I don't know" need not be a final destination. After several tries with "I don't know" answers, when I suggest that, "I don't know" is a cop-out, clients push through the roadblock and come up several ideas. Then moments later, a string of viable ideas come forth, as they accept that they can really figure it out.

Ask yourself the question, "If you did know, what would you have?" Try this with some of your team members. Ask them, "What might you think about this situation if you did know?" and see what reaction you get.

One more angle on setting intent has to do with our emotional reactions in leadership situations. A common situation that people bring into the coaching conversation is that they tend to get angry or frustrated, and visibly show those emotions when they are in meetings or interacting with individuals. Their request of the coaching process is to help them not react, or to help them hide the reaction. We can certainly do that, and in some cases we do, particularly when those situations are acute.

But I almost always invite people to consider another approach, and to think differently about the underlying situation. If they can get in touch with what's causing the emotional reaction in that moment, they have the opportunity to consider changing their intent about what they want to have happen. Let me get a little more specific.

If we're in a meeting and someone is continually challenging us, and we are finding ourselves getting more and more frustrated and angry, can we reframe our intent? What if our intent was no longer to argue with this person, but instead to truly understand why they see things so differently, and are so passionate about that difference in perspective?

What if we become the expert investigator? What if we are able to draw them out and engage them in a series of questions in an inquiry process, whereby we could thoroughly understand their point of view, perhaps even better than they do?

Would that change our emotional reaction? Would we cease being angry and frustrated? Would we, in fact, show up as curious, fully engaged, and interested in the other individual and what their thought process is?

I think most of us readily see that we would have a significant shift in energy and that our emotional response would change. We would no longer have to control our anger, because our anger and our frustration would cease to exist. This is often the approach that we encourage our coaching clients to experiment with, as part of managing or changing their intent.

In the May 25th, 2011 issue of CIO Magazine, there was an article by a former CIO and CFO of the Coca-Cola Company. The title of the article, "Leaders Intuition," with the subtitle, "Many highly educated people have had their intuitive leadership abilities trained out of them." In the article, Jack Bergstrand asserted that, "...effective leadership is fairly straightforward," and presents "four key leadership behaviors...that can accelerate sustainable innovation and transformation."

I fully agree with both assertions that leadership is fairly straightforward and that much of our intuitive leadership has been trained out of us. I differ with Mr. Bergstrand a bit in the selection of the four key behaviors, and I'd like to summarize the process of setting our intent with some of the keys to intuitive leadership as we've discussed them in this chapter:

1. **It's not enough to be right, we also need to be helpful.** In today's world of limitless data and information, many of us can be right or make the case for being so. In taking the step beyond being "right" to crafting a truly "helpful" solution or approach, we are more likely to inspire others as leaders to follow us.

2. **Clarify our intent before speaking or acting.** When we know exactly what we want to accomplish and why we want it, we are much more likely to speak and behave effectively. For example, are we trying to convince someone to see a situation our way? Or are we trying to deepen our relationship with them?

3. **Ask more and tell less.** When we ask questions of others, we engage with them much more deeply than when we tell them "how it is." We also increase the

likelihood that we will learn more than if we hadn't asked. This works as well when we ask questions of ourselves, rather than give in to our unconscious self-talk.

4. **Use "Yes" to empower your "No."** When we need to say "No," first say "Yes" to shared values, then say "No" to the specific request and how it conflicts with those shared values. Finally, say "Yes" to alternatives that are better aligned with those values.

And, as an additional bonus point:

5. **Treat "I don't know" as a transition to another idea, and not the end of our thought process.** When we hear or utter the words, "I don't know," then ask, "OK, so how do we figure it out?" and keep the thought process going.

In truth, there are many additional intuitive practices that enable us to be more effective leaders. I hope that if you have your favorites, you would consider sharing them by emailing or posting comments to our website, at www.Kantor-ConsultingGroup.com/AskBob.

Now let's move on to the next step in the Simple Leadership Life Cycle, the process of Prioritization.

Chapter Four
Prioritization and Time Management
Or, "It' not enough to do things right, we also need to do the right things."

We don't approach leadership coaching with an agenda or with a specified curriculum. We do tailor every program and conversation to each individual and where they are in their leadership challenges in the moment. As part of my diagnostic work at the beginning of a coaching relationship, I inquire about the type of hours my client works.

Some time ago I was working with a client who averaged 12 hours a day, five days a week in the office, and he typically put in another hour to an hour and a half later in the evening at home, plus two to four additional hours each weekend.

When I asked if this was a practice that he wanted to continue, I was quite surprised. He responded with a question of his own, "Why would I not want to continue that?"

I asked him if working an average 10-hour day might be something that he would want to consider doing. His immediate answer was, "No, why would I want to consider doing that?"

We discussed the benefits of working a 10-hour day and the possible consequences of continuing his current practice. We had this conversation, based upon his values, before we addressed the question of feasibility and practicality.

We first explored what the benefits might be to him as a person. There was the question of his general health, his energy levels during the day, his overall creativity, and his ability to handle stressful situations. Then we took a look at the impact on his life outside of his business role; his life at home. We looked at his role as a spouse, his relationship with his wife, his responsibilities and chores as co-leader in the home environment, his tasks and routines in daily life and the challenges around the house.

We did the same for his roles and responsibilities as the parent of two children, one almost a teen and the other a young teenager. He had a very warm, loving relationship with both of his children and was striving to be actively engaged in their weekend and afterschool activities.

This client also had a fairly important and robust role as the adult child of two aging parents, one of whom had very significant health and healthcare challenges. He helped both parents manage the care and treatment of the one that was ailing. And because of their challenges, the other parent was not well positioned to carry the load that the less healthy parent required.

Next we looked at the implications for the company for which he worked. One of the questions that I posed was about the impact on the people in his organization that he led, and the message he was sending them based on the example he was setting as the leader.

He said, "Well, everyone has to work hard, but I don't expect anyone to work the same hours that I do."

We went back and forth a bit to compare and contrast the message that he was intending to send to the people in his organization, versus the message he was actually sending. This came down to the distinction between what we do as leaders, compared to what we say as leaders. As we all know, actions so often speak louder than words.

He realized that this could create confusion and stress, and even some interpersonal conflict in his organization. Some of the individuals were following the behavioral lead that he was setting, and working very long hours on a regular basis. While others were striving for, and claiming, what they felt was a more rational work/life balance and working an average of "only" 10 hours a day.

That created quite a bit of dissention in his organization. Those who were working longer hours expected those who were working shorter hours to be more like them. And, those who were working shorter hours grew increasingly frustrated with the "unreasonable expectations" from those who were working the longer hours.

Finally, we concluded our exploration of the pros and cons of reducing the daily average hours worked from 12 to 10-hours a day. We took a look at the capacity that he had for situations that truly required the extra effort, in terms of longer days, which might be 12, 14 or in some cases, 16 hours.

It quickly became clear to him that his resilience and capacity for those unusual, but not infrequent situations that required very long days, would be limited. If an external business situation arose that warranted a 14 or 16-hour day, for more than one or two days in a row, he didn't have the endurance to put in the extended hours.

Let's move on from the story, to the details of how to more effectively lead with better Prioritization and Time Management.

Let me be frank and share that this is one of my favorite

topics in leadership development coaching for many reasons:

- In every one of the hundred-plus people that I have coached over the past two years, all of them have claimed that they had a time management challenge.

- Improvements in Prioritization and Time Management have a huge impact on everything that we do as leaders. It also has a huge effect on our job satisfaction, our work/life balance, and on our overall stress levels.

- Massive improvements are very simple to make. As we get into the tools and technique section in this chapter, you will see that for yourself and hopefully agree.

- Skill improvements in Prioritization and Time Management generalize to every other aspect of our lives. I will demonstrate that leadership is not a business-specific skill that only returns benefits when we are in the workplace doing our jobs. In fact, leadership is a critical success component in all aspects of our lives. I maintain that Prioritization and Time Management pay huge dividends in our leadership at home, as volunteers in community organizations, and even when we're simply participating in a community meeting. We may not have a leadership position or a title, but we do have occasional opportunities to provide leadership to the larger body during the course of the meeting or proceedings.

- In 15% to 20% cases where a business coaching client tells me that the coaching has changed their lives, it is frequently as a result of their improvements in how they approached Prioritization and Time Management.

I could go on and list many more, but this makes my point. I hope this is one area that will become one of your favorites, as well.

In the past couple of years, every one of my coaching clients has told me they have a problem with Time Management. I always challenge them. I ask how much of the problem that they perceive as one of not having enough time, may actually be a reflection of challenges that they have with the way they Prioritize their work and how they actually spend their time.

With a bit of reflection, many of them acknowledge that constantly changing priorities, and/or lack of clarity around priorities, is an root cause of what they typically experience as Time Management challenges.

I maintain that we find time for everything that we consider a priority. When we feel that we don't have enough time, it is often because we have not done an effective job of establishing, protecting and addressing our priorities. This applies to priorities we to tasks, as well as to time, where we allocate time in response to all the tasks that we choose to address during a day.

With that as background, let's think about Focus as part of Prioritization. Think in terms of the diffused light from the sun as it filters through the atmosphere, sometimes through haze and clouds, and warms us and the entire planet. Contrast that to what happens when that same sunlight is focused on through a magnifying glass.

For those of you who, as children, played with focusing

sunlight through a magnifying glass, I think you would readily acknowledge that such focused sunlight is incendiary, and goes way beyond being warm.

I realize that my experience as a boy growing up in the United States is not typical for people from many other parts of the world. For those who have not had the experience of taking a simple magnifying glass and focusing the sun's rays through it, either on a match head or a piece of paper, let me share the experience from my childhood.

When we were kids, we had an inexpensive magnifying glass from the local toy store. We would sit on the sidewalk on a sunny afternoon and take a match from a matchbook, or a piece of paper, and focus the sunlight on it. Within seconds, the match head would ignite, setting the entire match aflame, or the piece of paper would start to brown and then smoke. If there were no clouds and the air was truly clear, even the piece of paper would go up in flames very quickly.

Focus, whether it's the sun's light through a magnifying glass, or our own attention through Prioritization of our work and time, can yield incendiary results in terms of our effectiveness.

Very often in our coaching conversations, we talk about Prioritization, or what is or is not worth doing. My clients will invariably say, "Well, I guess I have to find time for that."

I always push back there and bring up the distinction between finding time and making time. There are specific reasons for this.

- When we think in terms of finding time, we are avoiding the responsibility and accountability for making time.

- I've yet to observe anyone finding time anywhere. Time is not hiding under a rock or the pile of papers on the upper left hand corner of our desks. Time is constantly flowing around us, and can be either applied in a focused way or squandered via diffusion or lack of focus.

- When we think in terms of *finding* time, we see the situations and challenges around us as out there and beyond our control. When we think in terms of *making* time, we see the situation as under our control, and within us rather than out there. This gives us a more intentional view of the situation so that we can be responsible for our response to it.

If you recall from Chapter Three, on setting our intent and being intentional, that is what I'm referring to here. When we believe that we make time for those activities that are priorities, then we are able to respond to the situation around us with the intent of achieving specific outcomes. That's how all of this ties together.

Hopefully by now, after having beaten you over the head with my 2x4 on the importance of Prioritization, its impact on Time Management, and the broad nature of the opportunity and the challenge, let's look into one approach for prioritizing our energy and time effectively.

I refer to this approach as the 3-20 List, 3-20 Model, or 3-20 Process. For those familiar with Stephen Covey's work and *The 7 Habits of Highly Effective People*, this is a logical extension of his "First Things, First" habit.

What I suggest to people is that the first step is to create a list of no more than 20 important tasks, activities or results that they need to achieve in the near future. Some people find that 10 is the right number for them, while others find that 15 or 20 works well for them. For anyone who tells me there are well over 20 on their list, we actually have a different conversation at that point, because I maintain that they don't have enough focus or clarity around what their roles and responsibilities are.

Step One

Create a list of no more than 20 items that are important to achieve in the near term or couple of days or weeks. In some cases, depending on the nature of your work, it may even be a couple of months, but it generally is not your annual list of priorities.

Here in the coaching conversation, many people inquire as to whether this is a task list, and if so, how it relates to their to-do list. For clarity, this is not your to-do list of the things that you want to do during the day. These are the important things that you need to get done, based upon what it is you're trying to accomplish and the value that you need to deliver to your company, based on your role and responsibility.

Step Two

Force rank the items on the list. A lot of people would normally indicate one of three levels of priority to the items on the list: high priority, medium priority, and low priority. (Why anyone would keep track of a low priority item on this list confuses me. You might consider removing any low priority items from the list before going further.)

It's not unusual to find that more than half the items on the list get an high priority. When we have more than a couple of high priorities, we really have no priorities. When everything is a high priority we, in fact, have no priorities.

Forced ranking is a process that requires you to assign a rank of 1 to the top priority, to only one item, on your list. And then the second next priority gets a 2, the third a 3, and so on. It is not allowable to repeat any of the numbers. When you try this, if you are like many clients, it's going to be severely tempting to assign several number 1's, several number 's, and so on. Please, don't do it. You'll see in a moment why that actually negates the entire value of the process.

I will warn you that simply making the decision about which item is number 1 and which item is number 2, can be an extreme challenge until you have developed muscles for making these distinctions.

(Remember our earlier discussion about the discomfort of making changes to our leadership behavior, and working through that discomfort for a long enough period of time – up to 30 days - to make that new behavior a comfortable new habit?)

The only way to develop these muscles is to practice. This process is often stressful and creates a lot of tension. Some people will initially insist that it just cannot be done, because everything on the list needs to get done. We will address that towards the end of this discussion, and then in more depth in the next chapter, which is about Delegation. (Hint, hint, big clue right here.)

You must force rank everything from 1 to 20, or to whatever number of items you have on your list. And yes, there will be times when it is painful and difficult to actually do that. There may even be times when you don't know how to force rank some of the items on the list. This is a wonderful mechanism for gaining clarity before committing your limited time and energy to action.

But if you really don't know the relative importance of item A to item B or to item C, then do additional research. Go back to some of your key stakeholders, your boss perhaps, other requesters or key leaders in the organization, and explore relative priority so you can do this step of this prioritization process effectively.

Step Three

This next step is admittedly optional, but one of my clients started to do this and immediately saw tremendous benefit. Put a date on each item when you first add it to your list. I too have integrated this practice with great benefit.

To add some clarity here on the process: This is a rolling list, a living list, if you will. If I make the list on January 15, by January 21 there may be some new priorities that need to appear on the list; some items that had been priorities on January 15 may not be the same level of priority or relative priority by January 21. That also implies that as you complete items on the list, they come off and other items can take their place.

As situations change, you may need to re-rank the prioritization based upon changing business circumstances, or a change of priorities by some of your key stakeholders who are in a position to have that leverage.

Step Four

This next step in the process should be done at least once a day. For some of us it's done first thing in the morning. For others it's one of the last things we do in the evening before we call it a day. In some cases, it's done at home before we call it a night.

Take a look at the list and be clear as to what the first, or top three priorities are, because that day, the following day, or in the morning, the process requires that you focus your time and energy on these, and minimize the amount of time that you spend on ancillary activities.

For instance, you don't spend two hours clearing your inbox or following up on email or returning phone calls first thing in the morning. You do need to be realistic and scan your emails, as there will be some that truly need to be addressed right away. The same might be true of voicemail and some other activities depending upon the nature of your work.

However, the key here is to spend as little time as possible first thing in the morning on those ancillary to-dos, so that you can focus on the top one, two, or three items on your 3-20 List. I ask every one of my clients how much time they can reasonably expect to devote in a morning, or over the course of a day, to those top items on their list based upon the nature of their work environment. Some of us have environments or jobs and responsibilities, that are by definition much more interrupt driven than others, and can therefor devote less time to our own agendas.

And yes, this 3-20 Process, and Prioritization and Time Management, is about minimizing the disruptions and driving our agendas based upon what we are striving to accomplish, rather than have our time and agendas driven by everyone else with whom we interact. The purpose here is for us to focus our time, based upon our strategic assessment of business priorities. (My colleague Brendon Burchard says, "Beware of your inbox, it's nothing but a convenient organizing system for other people's agendas.")

However, realistically, some of us can't muster more than 30 minutes of focus time a day. Most of us can muster one or two hours each day, and unless we are very high up in the organization hierarchy, it's been my experience that few of us can really muster more than two or three hours a day working on items on this list.

If you can spend more than two or three hours, definitely go for it. If you can do it a couple of days a week, but not every day of the week, definitely go for it. I find that one or two days a week I can spend the bulk of my day working on the top of my 3-20 List, but some days, I too am limited to about two or three hours a day. And there are some days when I really can't get to it at all. I assume the same will be true for many of you.

That is the practice. Each day work on the things that are the most important and reprioritize at least once a day. The reality is that by putting in focused time on your top priorities, you will find that you are delivering much more value in the short term, and certainly over the long term, than if you don't apply a process along these lines.

This is one reason why many of my clients tell me this has changed their lives. They find that not only are they delivering much higher value, but to their surprise, they experience a much lower level of stress. They also find that they are much more comfortable with what they are doing, are much better at interacting with people around them, and are much improved at managing interruptions. They also find that the example they are setting for the people on their teams, has a very strong trickledown effect, so that their entire organization becomes more effective and delivers more value.

There will be items, particularly if you're keeping a running list of about 20, that never rise to the top of the list. That can be a good thing, and you may need to make a decision about those items after a certain period of time. If those items never rise to the top of the list, do they need to be done? Or, did they make it onto the list because, at the time that they came up they seemed like important things to do with high value returns. But then as time progressed, it became apparent that what appeared important in the moment really wasn't that important in the long term? If that's the case, drop them off the list and you're done with them.

That's one reason why it's helpful to put the date on items when we put them on our list. For anything that's more than a month old that hasn't made it to the top of the list, I encourage people to either drop it from the list or move to the next step of the Leadership Life Cycle, which is Delegation.

There will be items that don't make it to the top of your list, but still need to get done. It's clearly not one of *your* priorities, and if it's been a month, it probably won't ever become one of your priorities. And yet, somebody has to do it. Therefore, that item is a great candidate to delegate to someone else in your organization.

I am not suggesting that items that don't rise to the top of your prioritization list, but have to get done, should be done by you just because their due dates are approaching.

This is a critical success factor for leaders. One of the reasons this model and process yields such high value results, is because all too often we find ourselves dragged into doing work because the item has a due date. Though it is not a high priority use of our time or attention, we do it because it has to get done.

By using this kind of a mechanism to filter and assess, it helps us get very, very clear on the types of activities that we really should be delegating to others in our organization. If you're thinking, "There isn't anyone in my organization who can do that even though it's not one of my priorities," then please stay with us and read the chapter on Delegation. We've got an answer for that as well.

Another question that often comes up around the use of this kind of a process is whether it's better to have one list or two lists.

If you recall, I said that these are not supposed to be to-do lists. That implies that most of us who use the 3-20 Model will have two lists. One of them will be the 3-20 with the important tasks and the other one will be our quick or urgent tasks that we keep track of on the to-do lists.

I have had clients very successfully use both approaches; one being a single list and the other being two separate lists. The ones who are successful with one list do it so the important tasks don't get lost to the quick or urgent tasks. They find that by having one list, it is easier and simpler to manage their time. Whereas, if they have two lists, it's easy for them to lose track of the 3-20 List and spend the entire day on their to-do list.

For those who prefer two lists, they find that the quick and urgent intems on their to-do list don't push the important items down their 3-20 List. In other words, they have found that with only one list, the phone calls, emails and so on wind up putting them right back to where they were before they had the 3-20 List. So the benefits of prioritizing and sorting the high priority items to the top of the list get lost when they use one list. They focus first on making progress on their top 3-20 List items, and later in the day address the items on their to-do list.

There you have it. There's no right answer, there's no one best way. I would suggest that you experiment and find what works best for you.

In creating their actual lists and and sorting tasks, I've seen people do this in several different ways.

Some people use email to create their list because their email systems give them a mechanism for prioritizing and indicating priority. Those who use email often do this on their smart phones.

Many of my clients like doing managing their list on a simple Excel spreadsheet, which can also be readily viewed and often maintained on a smart phone.

The mechanism is fairly simple. Use one column for each item on the list and then your forced ranking in a numerical column to the left. You can use the data sort option periodically to sort everything on the list based upon the forced ranking.

This may sound like a lot of busy work or administrivia, but please trust me. If you do this regularly for a couple of weeks, it begins to become second nature and moves very, very quickly.

Now, I owe it to everyone to fess up on something. There is a dark, dirty, little secret to this very wonderful technique. Because it is so concrete, this is one of the simplest tools and techniques in this entire book. And yet, it is one of the hardest to apply consistently, because it goes against the way we are hardwired.

What do I mean by that?

In the business world, we often believe, and our values

support the belief, that success requires that we do everything on our plates and get it all done. If we don't do everything, we often feel inadequate and unsuccessful. As you apply the 3-20 Process, there will definitely be important items that you don't get done. Even if they're on the list they will not all get done, as we discussed earlier.

In order for us to feel good about applying this process, we need to choose to recognize and accept (notice I did not say "have to...") that in today's world there are always going to be more demands on our time and our attention than we will ever be able to address. Our success truly requires that we effectively and aggressively filter out the less important demands, and focus first on the most important ones.

Failure to filter along these lines sub-optimizes our effectiveness, and failure to accept that reality saps our energy and our enthusiasm.

Have you ever had the experience where you have been very busy all day long and gotten a lot done? And then when you get home that evening, it occurs to you that even though you had a great day and you got a ton of stuff done, you didn't get several things done that really would have had the greatest impact on what you are trying to accomplish in the near term?

Most of us talk about this like, "I ran around all day like a chicken without a head and I didn't get anything done." If that rings a bell, and I expect it does, I strongly encourage you to try to focus on applying a tool or a technique like this.

The other reason that I encourage people to strive to overcome the initial difficulty in applying this very simple process, is because it has such a large impact on the lives of my clients who do stick with it.

I am frequently reminded of how important this very simple process is when clients tell me that this technique has changed their life, or how their days and weeks are significantly improved, or they are getting recognized for new levels of value that they are contributing to their organization.

Let's now shift gears away from the 3-20 Process and come back to the idea of Prioritization as separate from Time Management.

When I told the story about focusing the sun's warmth through a magnifying glass and creating incendiary energy — that was about focus. One of the challenges that we have with maintaining our focus, once we have prioritized our work, is the constant voice inside of our head that often distracts us.

We may be in the middle of being productive, working on one of our top priorities, when the voice in our head raises its volume and suggests we answer an email. So as not to forget to do that item, we stop what we're doing and reply to the email.

But more often than not, this voice is unnecessarily worrisome, inaccurate and tends to pull us off center away from tasks we chose to be doing based upon our prioritization process.

An exercise that several of my clients have found very helpful is to take a period of time to pay attention to this self-talk. By doing this they can become aware of areas of their practice and leadership that they may need to pay more attention to.

The exercise is fairly simple. For those who might benefit from this, but hesitate to try it because it sounds like mediation, please give it a try. This is not meditation. This is a way to focus our concentration to get a better read on what that self-talk is really addressing.

I encourage people to find a quiet place. Maybe close their eyes, maybe not. Take a couple of deep breaths. This is not a deep breathing exercise, just a couple of deep breaths. Then breathe normally. On the first inhale of the exercise, count 50, on the first exhale count 49, on the next inhale count 48; the idea being to count down from 50 to zero.

If you are like most people, I can almost guarantee that the first couple of times you do this exercise, you won't get to below 40, and that's okay. This is not about getting to zero. It's about recognizing when we have lost the count.

What typically happens is you'll be counting 47, 46, 45, and the next thing you know you are in the middle of thinking about something else and then you realize that you have stopped counting. At that moment, take a look at what it is that you're thinking about, make a mental note of it and then go back to counting.

This is not meant to take the better part of the day, but can be done in the space of just a few minutes. In fact, you can generally do this exercise in no more than five to seven minutes.

If you get lost in your self-talk, the exercise can actually take longer because initially you can be lost in thought for anywhere from 5-15 minutes before you realize that you have lost the count.

After doing this a couple of times each day for several days, my clients begin to see patterns that have been distracting them. This enables them to either put some of these distractions on the 3-20 List and address them in a structured and focused fashion, or just heighten their awareness of how distracting this self-talk can be. This awareness causes them to be less sensitive and responsive to self-talk that previously was a big distraction.

As such, it's another way to build our muscles of more effective leadership skills.

I encourage you to try this as a way to enhance your awareness of what is distracting you from the focus that you need to prioritize your work and practice effective time management.

Let's move on to another practice that so many of my clients find effective. How often do you find yourself looking at something that requires your attention and asking yourself, "Hmmm, do I have to do this?" Or how often do you look at something and say, "Man, this is not important. This is not high value, but darn I have to do it."

I would encourage you to try to develop what I call the "have to" filter. And any time you find yourself thinking, "I have to," stop and ask yourself some questions.

Why do you have to? Who says that you have to? Do you really have to? Do you choose to?

Sometimes we feel that we have to do something and in reflection and further examination we will realize that we also choose to, in which case is no longer an "I have to."

Should you choose to? Sometimes we wind up with tasks that we first think that we have to. We then decide that we would prefer not to, but as part of the Prioritization we realize that we should choose to.

And then, if you really have to and/or should, does it have to be you? And if the answer is "no," move on to the Delegation chapter that follows this one.

If you believe that it shouldn't have to be you, but unfortunately, right now it does because there's no one who can handle it for you to delegate it to. Similar to the statement I made about five pages or so ago. Move on to the Delegation chapter and let's work on how you can improve your ability to delegate to others in your organization.

Another tip about Prioritization and Time Management: Very often we find ourselves spending a lot of time on specific tasks on a repeating basis. For many of us, particularly in the business world, that's email. We get so many messages that if we hope to stay current on our communications with stake holders and colleagues, we find ourselves spending hours each day reading and responding to email.

I invite you to consider putting a time limit on those kinds of tasks. I suspect that you've heard the idea that work tends to expand to the amount of time that we allocate to it. Consider applying the converse, and to be more directive in terms of your focus on Time Management.

If you typically average four hours a day responding to email, cut it back to three and give yourself a hard stop. Actually keep track of this with a timer and when you get to the three-hour mark, or whatever the target you set, stop working on email until the next day. Do that for a couple of days and then continue to set the bar lower every couple of days. I have seen people cut the time they devote to email by 50% within several weeks or a couple of months.

Based upon what I have seen my clients accomplish, I can assure that you will begin to get the same amount of work done in shorter periods of time and, in many cases, will produce better and higher quality work.

Begin to pay attention to how much time you spend on one-on-one conversations, performance feedback conversations, conducting design or project reviews, or anything that you do on a regular basis, and work incrementally to reduce time spent on those activities. I promise that your effectiveness and productivity will go up.

Another significant challenge related to focus, is handling what can be constant interruptions. We certainly can't eliminate all of the interruptions, but one area that we typically all struggle with is interruptions by members of our organization.

Many of my clients use a fairly common practice that they call office hours. And they actually do it in two very opposite ways. Some of them establish office hours as private time during which they prefer not to be interrupted.

This was the way I used to do it myself, when I worked in a large organization. I let my team know that 11:00 to 12:00 in the morning was my private time, and unless something truly urgent came up, I preferred that they not interrupt me. Very quickly people learned to honor my request for my private office hours. That often gave me at least an hour of very focused time to work on items on my 3-20 List items.

A lot of people do just the opposite. They establish office hours and deliver the message to their team that they prefer 'stop bys' and 'drop ins' during these specific office hours, thereby freeing up blocks of time when they can focus on their top priorities.

What you can afford to allocate as either private time or office hours will be very individualistic, based upon the nature of your work and the organizational culture within which you work. I encourage everyone to apply some form of office hours as a way to enhance their focus and ability to prioritize.

To close this chapter, let's come back to the story with which we opened it. Many of us reduce our productivity as a result of forcing ourselves into a work day that is much too long. We tend to get lazy when we allow 10-12-hour days to become our normal routine. If we believe that we're going to be in the office until 7:00 or 7:30 at night, that actually encourages us to be less efficient during the day.

Work expands to fill the available time. The process of giving yourself shorter and shorter amounts of time to do regular work, such as managing email, can be an effective way to regain time for important priorities during the day. The same is true when deciding whether or not to work at home in evenings and on weekends.

Practice making decisions sooner and faster with less data, and overall spend less time making decisions. Later we will address how to do that, as well as doing better risk reward assessments, in terms of which decisions require extra time and more data.

Prioritize more and more often by using tools like the 3-20. Delegate more often. Focus more intently. Use office hours. And, continually challenge yourself to do the most important things in less time.

Let's move on to Delegation as another way to support our improvement in prioritization, focus, and time management.

Chapter Five
Delegation
Or, "It's not enough to get stuff done, we also need to grow our people."

In the last chapter on Prioritization and Time Management, we referred to the importance of Delegation to allow the possibility of focusing time and energy on the top priority items on your 3-20 List. By delegating activities that need to be done to deliver results, to other people in your organization, you can insure that the items that don't make it to the top of your list still get done in the timeframes necessary.

Sometimes we feel challenged by this because we are concerned that people in our organizations don't have the skills necessary to accomplish the tasks we choose to delegate. In this chapter we will focus on *what* and *how* to delegate, so our staff can deliver the results that we expect. The focus here will be on techniques to ensure that they *can* deliver the desired results.

In the next chapter, we will actually focus on techniques to ensure that they *will* and *do* deliver.

The first half of delegation is:

- How do we identify what we need to delegate?

- How do we determine whom we can delegate to?

- What are some of the approaches to delegation, so that the people to whom we delegate have a good probability to succeed with the work that we're delegating?

Here's a quick story about how this played out for one of my clients in my leadership coaching program. I was working with a manager of a software development group, and in this organization one of the primary activities for the software development teams was what they called ticket management. Any questions from external clients or internal key stakeholders about how or whether the system was working, if there were malfunctions or bugs, as well as small enhancement requests, came through a centralized ticketing system.

Each day, this manager spent hours going through the new tickets determining: 1) what category of work they fell into, 2) who on the team had the expertise to address the issue, and 3) who had bandwidth to address the ticket item. Each day the manager also spent time following up on tickets in various stages of completion. As you can imagine, ticket management was a lot of work. Additionally, the manager did strategic product planning, oversaw new product development activities, managed staff, staff development, and often worked 11-12 hour days.

This manager's plate with more than full, so the question I posed was, "What takes a significant amount of your time that you could delegate?" In many situations where we do mid-level management coaching, often the manager's initial response is, "If there were anything else that I could delegate, I would have already delegated it."

We took a step back and looked at it from a slightly different perspective. We asked ourselves, "If there were no limitations of skills and capabilities of the members of his team, what would be the best activity to delegate?" We were looking for an activity that was not the best use of his time, and something that would be interesting and challenging to someone else on his team—an opportunity to develop new skills and perhaps enhance their career.

The ticket management function was the most likely situation or task to delegate. When we discussed the viability of doing that, the manager expressed concern that nobody on his team currently had the skill or experience to manage the ticket queue. When we looked closely at his staff, we agreed that if anyone could do the task, it would be his second-in-command, who was also his back-up when he was not in the office.

Next we explored what it would take for that individual to be able to handle ticket management to a reasonable level of effectiveness. The conclusion was that with some real-time mentoring, his second-in-command could come up to speed and learn to effectively manage the ticket queue, perhaps in a period of about two months.

Given how many hours per day that he was currently spending doing the ticket management himself, he came up with an approach whereby he could mentor his second-in-command to do the work with him, in about the same amount of time that it was taking him to do it by himself.

With that approach, he made the commitment to begin working with his colleague and see if within two months he could ensure that his colleague could effectively handle the task. This would free him up to do some of the more strategic and higher leverage work that he felt was appropriate for his role and responsibility in the organization.

Once they started this mentoring process, it took just over two weeks to bring his second-in-command up to speed to take over the task. With two weeks of careful attention, focus and working together, they both agreed that his second-in-command was more than ready to take over. And while the manager stayed close to the situation while his colleague began to handle the task on his own, both of them quickly realized that the mentoring had been quite successful and complete.

The level of performance on the ticket management task was certainly more than adequate. The risk of significant error, after two and one-half weeks, was quite low. And, the colleague continued to learn and solidify his expertise so further mentoring was unnecessary. By the end three weeks the manager had freed up two to three hours a day to address the more important work he had to do.

This example illustrates the most important theme around delegation that I see and address in my leadership development coaching. Very often as leaders, we underutilize the capacity of our people and don't delegate higher level or additional work, as quickly and as often as we can.

As a result of coaching, clients extend themselves and delegate more work, either of a nature they felt could not be delegated, or to individuals they had been concerned were not ready for that work. Very often they are pleasantly surprised that the individuals deliver more value and achieve better results than they had expected. That illustrates one of the misconceptions about delegation that most leaders have. Many leaders believe that delegation is something that we do when we have trained and developed one or more on our team to be 100% ready to take on a new task. My clients prove this to be true all the time. There is as much to be gained from delegation as a professional development tool, as there is to be gained from using delegation as a way to free up managerial and leadership time.

I see regular evidence that using delegation as a way to develop new skills and capabilities in our staff, is often a more effective training and development methodology than the more traditional training that we do within our corporations.

It is beyond the scope of this book to go into all of the reasons why, but I would suspect that many of us could intuitively agree that hands-on, on-the-job training frequently has a higher value than classroom training. When you come out of the classroom, you then have to begin applying what you learned; whereas with on-the-job training, you are constantly applying what you are learning in the very specific context in which it needs to be applied.

With that as the framework, let's explore how to leverage delegation as a way to free up our own time and energy based upon better prioritization, but also as a way to accelerate the movement of lower value work from ourselves to various staff members. (Please note I used the phrase "lower value" and not "low value." Low value work should not be delegated. It should be eliminated.)

We need to clarify for ourselves, as well as our staff, that by delegating work we are not washing our hands of the responsibility for the outcome of that work. Sometimes I see that leaders hesitate to delegate work because they are concerned that they are taking too big of a risk, in terms of the bottom line business impact. And, while we certainly don't want to delegate complex work to inexperienced professionals, nor do we want to "throw it over the wall."

There are ways in which to delegate work so that complete and adequate control is still retained, and risk is minimized. One of the first steps is to be clear, for both the manager doing the delegation and for the staff member picking up the assignment, that we are delegating the work and some degree of responsibility for doing the work. But at the end of the day, the manager always remains accountable for the results being achieved.

Certainly, as effective leaders, we would never throw our colleague under the bus and say to upper management that it wasn't our fault that our colleague didn't meet our expectation or missed a deadline. So, again, the first step is to be clear that we can delegate the responsibility for doing the work, but not the accountability for delivering the result.

There is implies that as part of delegating work, and also in then managing the work after it's been delegated, that we will stay in regular communication with the person or people to whom we have delegated the task. It's important that everyone understand that is going to happen, so no one is uncomfortable with the ongoing communication. When that doesn't go well, or when expectations aren't met, we hear staff members complaining about being micromanaged, because his manager hasn't let go of the task. We will address that in more detail later in this chapter.

We talked about using delegation as a way to develop or stretch people, and there's a continuum that I find very helpful when working with clients on this. When we are looking at delegating a task to an individual, one of the first things we need to do is to assess their current skill level at it is related to doing that work.

If we have a relatively senior individual who is totally or nearly capable of doing the work, as the work is currently structured, then the amount of support that we provide would be significantly less than if we were delegating to a more junior person with a lower skill level. We must be aware of the development gap as we determine how much support will be necessary for them to successfully take on the delegated task.

Given the case of a senior person who is fully competent to do the task, the delegation process would be shorter and quicker. We wouldn't tell the individual what or how to do it; nor would we telling the individual the time frame within which it would be appropriate to complete the task. We might give them a quick description of what needs to be done or the result to be delivered, and then ask them a series of questions about how they were going to go accomplish it, how long it was going to take, and what challenges or issues they saw.

The operative word, to summarize the process for delegating to more experienced people, is "Ask". I'm describing what I call the "Ask-Tell continuum" which is a continuum based upon the level of experience or knowledge of the person to whom we are delegating.

We need to be clear on our Intent (as discussed in Chapter 3) as part of leveraging this continuum. To what degree do we simply want to get something done, versus to develop staff? When we are more intent on simply getting something done, we are more likely to rely on or go to our more senior staff. When our intention is to develop staff, then we can go to the more junior or less experienced staff where the process of delegation is more robust, and leverages the "Tell" or telling portion of the continuum much more so than asking questions about how they will proceed.

We might be inclined to tell someone not only the result that needs to be delivered, but also outline the steps to go through and the general approach they might take, in terms of tools or technologies they might apply, and people to engage with and talk to. We would probably want to ask them to come back to us with their own estimate of how long it will take to complete the task after they take a reasonable amount of time to study the assignment and to review their approach to the project.

Notice it's not the nature of the task that determined whether we delegated it, or to whom we delegated it. The task was delegated and the decision about who to delegate to was a reflection of our intent. The person chosen to receive the assignment helped guide the process for doing the delegation.

With that in mind, the next question is how to do more delegation to free up even more time. I encourage clients to do a variation of their 3-20 List and make a separate list of everything that they could delegate. Even better would be to use the original 3-20 List, and force rank it based on ability to delegate from easy to difficult, rather than the importance of getting it done. By doing this, you now have a high level plan for implementing a delegation program. I encourage people, at the very least, to start with delegating the first, or easiest item on that list.

An easy way to implement this is to take the easiest item to delegate, give it to the most competent or most experienced individual on the team, as chances are pretty good that the delegation: 1) happens very quickly, 2) is extraordinarily successful, and 3) doesn't require a whole lot of time and effort to follow up.

When we get a little more aggressive in the coaching process, I encourage my clients to either delegate several of the tasks from the top of the list, and/or to delegate at least one item on the list to each one of their direct reports. Depending upon the size of the team, that may result in three to twelve items to delegate. Realistically, it's not very reasonable to expect to delegate twelve items, one to each member of the team in a relatively short time frame, and still provide the necessary level of support and follow-up. But it is often very feasible to delegate 3-5 items from this list over a period of a couple of weeks.

At this point, you may be wondering:

- At what point does a manager stop delegating?
- Is there a danger that one can delegate so much of their work that they no longer have anything to do?

Let me address the latter question first, since the idea is somewhat amusing. Some time ago, after a client had gone through several iterations of this structured delegation process, he said, "Bob, I've got a problem." When I asked him what it was, he looked at me, laughed and said, "I have too much time on my hands right now. I don't know what to do with myself."

Needless to say, by the end of that 45-minute coaching session, he did more than address the question as to how he should be allocating his time. He went on to spend a large and very effective amount of time working closely with senior people in his organization, and together they came up with strategic direction for product and business development, which over time yielded increased revenue and product margins.

How do you know when to stop delegating? I suggest that you continue delegating until you get to a point where you need to take certain tasks back. This could be either because you have loaded all of your available recourses to the point where they can't handle any more work, or because some of the tasks that you have delegated prove to be beyond the capability or the skill level of certain members of your team.

In either one of those cases, you would prefer to continue to mentor your staff, both in terms of improving their skill level and making better use of their time around prioritization and time management. At the end of the day, however, if there are one or more delegated tasks that you feel need to come back to you for the time being, then you have reached the end of that process for the moment.

I know from experience with all of my clients, that they get a lot further with this delegation process than they initially thought they would.

There is another mechanism, or tool, that we can use when we think about delegating that will make us more comfortable when delegating to people who are not 100% "ready" to take on the work. It will also enhance the individual's own comfort level and awareness with how to succeed with the delegation process. It is the idea of *conscious and unconscious competence and incompetence,* which defines four stages of skill development that has been used in management and leadership development for many years.

In developing expertise and competence, most of us go through four stages of skill development:

- In the first stage, we are not aware of what we don't know. That is called *unconscious incompetence,* meaning we are not conscious of what we are not capable of doing. For someone who is unconsciously incompetent, it would not be a good idea to delegate a task to them that requires a skill they don't have and don't understand.

- The second stage in skill development is when we become *consciously incompetent*, which translates into, "We
know what we don't know." That is when we become
aware of a skill gap and we are then able to do development work to begin to close that gap.

Once we are consciously incompetent, we become a
candidate for taking on delegated work with a significant amount of support. That would be the example we
spoke about earlier in the "Ask/Tell continuum"; where if
I am consciously incompetent, then as long as you give
me enough direction by telling me what to do and how
to do it, I can begin to practice the skills necessary to do
the work and successfully deliver on the delegated task.
And as long as you stay close to the process to help me
see when I am off track, then I can successfully execute
and we can both be satisfied.

When we are very competent in executing a task and we
delegate it to someone who is now consciously incompetent, we will sometimes, after we outline everything that
they are going to do, leave them with the admonition, "If
you need any help, let me know." Unfortunately, when
an individual is not competent, or even consciously incompetent, they may not know when they need help,
and therefore, they get into trouble. When we finally circle back to them, we discover the trouble because we are
at a much higher level of competence. But by then it's too
late, the damage has been done. The project or the task
is either behind schedule or is having a quality problem.

When we are delegating work to someone who is consciously incompetent, we need to retain accountability

for tracking the success of their effort and not leave it to them to manage that themselves. I can't emphasize this enough. It's an area where most leaders struggle with delegation early on in their managerial careers, and it is the primary reason why, after someone tries delegating as a development effort, they pull back very, very quickly and claim that they tried it and it didn't work.

- As you practice a skill more and more, you move into the third stage of skill development, which we call *conscious competence*. At this stage you can do the tasks reliably and repeatedly, as long as you remain focused on the steps necessary to do it. The good news is that you can be counted upon to deliver the results and you feel comfortable and confident in delivering the results.

   The bad news is that if you become distracted, then your performance is likely to suffer. Distraction can come in many forms:

   - Being given too much work.

   - Being under too much pressure because of the profile of the task at hand.

   - Becoming ill. You may come down with a cold or flu and have difficulty concentrating.

   - A personal challenge or problem outside of work that distracts your attention and resiliency.

   There are many other potential distractions, but the point is that when somebody is consciously competent, leaders still need to provide a certain amount of task oversight to ensure that they and we are successful.

- Finally, the fourth level of professional development is

where you are competent and you no longer have to focus on how you do a task or what you do. We call this *unconsciously competent,* or the level of accomplishment of the expert. How often have you tried to learn how to do something from someone who is an expert? Very often that can be difficult, because once we become an expert, or have been an expert for a period of time (have practiced in the realm of *unconscious competence*) we forget how or why we do things, because we do them automatically or unconsciously.

When anyone reaches a point of expertise or unconscious competence, that's where delegation becomes the simplest to achieve, because at that point we are pretty much just tossing work over the fence, knowing that the individual who is taking it up has the skill and capability that they need, not only to get it done, but also to take corrective action when necessary and to know exactly when that is.

Using the conscious competence model is a way to determine what approach to delegation is most likely to be successful. It can be a very powerful tool to reduce the risk of delegation, and can enhance the experience that we and the people to whom we delegate have as part of the process.

Let's move on now to a couple of challenges that may arise as a result of delegating. I'm sure that all of us, at various points in our career, have either experienced a manager who micromanaged us, or been a manager who has received feedback from staff about being micromanaged.

I know I have certainly been told by staff at certain points in my career that I have a tendency to micromanage. What I learned from my own experience, is that when I am microman-aging, it is very often the result of my not having enough infor-mation about what's going on. This in turn leads my not feeling comfortable that the critical work that has been delegated is be-ing executed in a controlled fashion.

The feedback that I give to colleagues when that happens, and fortunately it does not happen (to me) very often anymore, is that when they feel that I am micromanaging, that means that they need to either figure out how to provide me with better or more effective information, and/or sit down with me to discuss how we better collaborate or communicate, so that I have the information necessary to be confident that the task at hand is under control.

When you find yourself micromanaging, please don't throw out the delegation baby with the bath water. Instead, come back to the processes and the tools that we've discussed in this chapter, and assess your delegation and management pro-cess. Allow yourself to continually improve those skills until you reach a point where delegation is working, both in terms of delivering the result, as well as having the people who are doing the work feel comfortable and confident with the way it is going.

Another challenge we sometimes face with delegation, particularly when someone is less experienced and stepping into a new role or assignment, is the "I don't know" response when we ask them how they might approach accomplishing the task. Sometimes the best way to deal with "I don't know," is to give them answers. Lead with the question or the "Ask" ap-proach, and if we discover that they don't have the expertise, move back into "Tell" and then share knowledge and expertise with them.

That's fine for one or two iterations. However, if after a couple of those we believe that the individual should probably have more of an idea by now, the first question you should ask yourself is, do they have the capacity to learn what you are trying to teach them? Assuming that they do, then it's more likely that they are simply lacking the confidence to move ahead, or are uncomfortable with what they perceive as a risk, and so respond with, "I don't know."

In this situation, encourage them not view that as the end of their thought process or your conversation. This is not the end of the line on our ability to figure out where to go next or how to move on. I would encourage you to either yourself answer the question, or ask your staff member the question: "What would happen if you thought instead, how do I figure it out?"

As we explored in an earlier chapter but is worth repeating here, what if "I don't know" were simply an acknowledgment that at that moment, and only at that moment, your team member didn't have a ready answer? Would that free him up to move on and continue to search for ideas, solutions and next steps, and/or, can you see yourself using that with your colleague to help them free up? I find that my clients almost always come up with useful ideas the moment they realize that "I don't know" need not be a final destination.

I encourage you to try this yourself and see what happens, and to certainly try it with your team members. Simply ask them, "What might you think if you did know?" and see what kind of reaction you get.

That pretty much sums up how to leverage delegation as both a professional development technique, as well as a way to

implement our own prioritization and time management decisions. Our focus was on how to approach and execute delegation, so that the people to whom we're delegating *can* do the
work that we are passing along to them.

In the next chapter, we will address the question of how
to continue that process, so that staff *will* execute effectively and
deliver the results that we want. We will call that Creating Conditions of Accountability.

Chapter Six
Creating Conditions of Accountability
Or, "It's not enough to delegate work, we also have to ensure it gets done."

In Chapter Five on Delegation, our focus was on delegating in such a way that our staff *can* successfully deliver the results that we are expecting. Here we will focus on techniques to ensure that our staff *will* and *does* deliver the results that we expect.

Creating Conditions of Accountability is also the platform upon which we build our techniques in the next chapter on Performance Management and Professional Development.

The foundation of this chapter is another simple, three-step process. The use of the word "simple" in our six-function Simple Leadership Life Cycle is a key component of this book and our philosophy. In our leadership coaching we focus on simple tools and techniques. Our belief and experience shows that it is enough of a challenge to change our behavior with simple models. And, it is much less likely that we will either make the change or even attempt the change if the models are complex.

With that in mind, here is the three-step process for creating conditions of accountability. We will then explore how to apply them.

Step One is to set clear and viable expectations with whomever we want to be accountable for delivering results. This might be a little hedge on the "three steps", because there are two pieces to it:

Part A is that the expectations need to be clear. While we will go into this in much more detail in Chapter Eight on Communication, we'll point out here that clarity is not simply a function of the message that we send or deliver. Clarity is also a function of how that message is received by the recipient. For now, just be aware that setting clear expectations requires an interaction and a level of engagement that we will cover in depth in Chapter 8.

Part B is viability. I'm sure that most of us have been in situations where someone higher up in the organization has come to us, asked us to do something, and with short notice to deliver it in an incredibly short period of time. Our immediate internal reaction is to gag, choke or let out a gasp, but the reality is that it's not possible, reasonable or viable.

If you've ever been in that situation, I'm sure you've experienced that there is a moment where you go through a quick assessment; Is it best to raise the issue about viability at that time, or let it go and simply do your best and deal with it later?

I suspect that you also may have had the experience where you asked someone to do something and given them an admittedly aggressive timeframe, and been relieved when they didn't push back. However, when you have given someone an aggressive timeframe and not had an explicit discussion about their belief about the viability of that timeframe, what has been your experience with the consistency of their delivery or the percentage of times that they actually met your expectations?

My own experience and that of hundreds of clients is that when we force people to accept conditions of viability that they question or are not comfortable with, there are times when they will deliver and meet those expectations. However, the level of commitment and the track record of delivery is certainly lower, than when there is consensus on the viability of the expectations.

Perhaps with our higher degree of experience, we may be more adept at providing estimates as to how long something should take. But at the end of the day, they are our estimate and not the estimate of the person we are going to hold accountable for doing the work. Therefore, best practice suggests that it is helpful to give the person whom we are holding accountable, an opportunity to provide their best estimate as to the viability of the task at hand, and what they feel is a reasonable time frame within which to deliver the expected results.

Once we have their assessment of viability, we can certainly engage in exploration with them as to how we might change the estimate so that it is better aligns with the business requirements at hand. Performance and accountability are best arrived at when there is shared agreement around the viability of the request.

In some cases, if the more experienced requester asks constructive questions about the individual's estimate around delivery, a misunderstanding can surface about the actual nature of the request. Perhaps the request is simpler and easier than the person who is going to do the work had understood. By going back and forth around viability, areas of confusion and simplification can be clarified.

Or, as sometimes happens as well, the person making the request doesn't have a thorough understanding about the work process involved to deliver the results that are being requested. Constructive conversation about the many steps to accomplish the task can often be helpful for the person making the request, to comfortably accept a longer timeframe or redefine the nature of the task so that it can be accomplished more quickly.

Step Two is to ensure that there are compelling consequences. When I say that to one of my clients, they immediately ask about the bounds or boundaries about creating negative consequences. I often point out that compelling consequences are not, by definition, always negative. It is perhaps even more important to establish compelling positive consequences.

All too often in today's work environment, with the tremendous pressure of expanded roles and responsibilities, we tend to focus entirely on avoidance of negative consequences. This can be somewhat effective in the short term, but over the long term does not lead to the most vibrant and effective of work environments. We have to create compelling positive consequences for meeting or exceeding expectations, and clear negative consequences for not meeting expectations.

Here there is a lot of latitude for creativity. It's easy to identify a negative consequence of poor performance with either informal or formal warnings, and how that might impact end of the year performance evaluation, merit raise and/or bonus. The flip side of that are the positive consequences of formal performance reviews, as well as merit raises and bonuses.

The reality is that, a) that typically occurs only once a year, and b) for many professionals in today's workplace, there is a limit as to how compelling the performance review and salary review can be.

I certainly don't intend to minimize the importance of monetary compensation. For professionals whose material needs are already met, money is an important measure of success; but in reality it does not have intrinsic motivating value. Based upon Maslow's Hierarchy of Need, if you're already making more than enough money to pay the bills, drive a nice car and send the kids to college, more money is better, but is limited in its ability to motivate one to overachieve.

In larger organizations, salary review is often regimented, and in smaller organizations frequently there isn't much free cash to reward people with salary. Often the person creating conditions of accountability has very real limits as to what they can do with monetary compensation or performance evaluation. Therefore, we need to get much more creative around establishing compelling consequences, both positive and negative, for performance. (This is only a foundation for Performance Management. We are on still on Step Two of Creating Conditions of Accountability.)

Negative Consequences

Sometimes when someone has made an error, creating compelling negative consequences can be as simple as providing negative feedback after a situation occurs. You can point out that, a) that shouldn't have happened, and b) the impact on the person who received or experienced the error is very often a significant issue.

Most of us are striving to do our best, most of the time. When we don't meet our own expectations and we hear about it, that can be very compelling. The flip side of that is also true as well, with the positive consequence.

Sometimes it is expected that we will always be right, we will operate error free, or we will always step up to any challenge. In today's fast-paced workplaces, the reality is that too often we don't recognize people with a simple thank you or acknowledgment of a job well done. This can be as simple as, "Thank you for going the extra mile," "Thank you for staying late," "Thank you for checking in over the weekend," or "Thank you for seeing this through, even though it impacted your weekend."

For many of us reward is also a function of recognition among our peers or our manager's Management. Having an accomplishment or a success called out during a team meeting or a staff meeting can be a compelling positive consequence.

Being given an opportunity to make a brief presentation at a staff meeting one or two levels up from our own department or organization can frequently be a positive consequence. Or, knowing that a mistake in a visible process was commented upon by a member of the management team can also be a very compelling negative consequence.

There are other ways that people get reward or recognition in our firms today. Another may be either earning a right to attend a meeting or a conference that the firm normally would not send us to. And the flip side of that is losing the opportunity to either attend an out of town conference or maybe a recruiting field trip, based upon not meeting expectations in our delivery of results. All of these present many combinations and permutations for how to create compelling consequences in support of creating conditions of accountability, apart from the more obvious annual salary adjustments.

Step Three in the process is to hold ongoing conversations based upon the facts, or empirical evidence. It is much more effective, when we are creating conditions of accountability, to be able to refer to facts and figures that everyone can agree upon and acknowledge are true, rather than to rely upon subjective beliefs.

For example, you might say, "You didn't deliver the result that I expected because I had to follow up too often with some of our key stakeholders." This is not as powerful or useful as, "You didn't meet my expectations. I was called in to six different meetings by our sponsors because you were not effectively keeping them in the loop about issues and issue resolution." In creating conditions of accountability, it is usually much more effective to have such a conversation after a first incident, rather than waiting until the situation gets worse.

Another example of ongoing conversations based upon the facts would be, "I just got a phone call from our key stakeholder on your project. He has called a meeting this afternoon that I will attend, because he is concerned that you are not addressing the issues and the challenges coming up in the project in an aggressive fashion. Let's talk about what's going on how you can address the situation differently."

Here's a quick review:

- **Step 1**: Set clear and viable expectations.
- **Step 2**: Create compelling consequences, both positive and negative.
- **Step 3**: Hold ongoing conversations based upon the facts.

I'd like to recognize two colleagues, Gregg Baron and Jeff Grimshaw, who shared this specific model with me. (For even more detail than we've covered here, see their excellent book, "*Leadership Without Excuses*.") I have been using it for over eight years, with hundreds of clients and in many situations. My clients have all experienced greater success when using this model.

Let's dig into some nuance around some specific techniques beyond what we've already discussed. We mentioned briefly in the Delegation chapter the idea of not telling staff how or by when to do things, instead focusing on what results are needed, and then allowing them to define the How and When. That certainly is an important technique around setting clear and viable expectations.

This has several advantages:

- It builds commitment.

- It encourages ownership.

- It allows staff to develop further skills during, or as a result of, the process of negotiating or clarifying expectations, as well as estimating what it takes to address those expectations.

- It also leverages team diversity and creativity.

We are all individuals, no matter how high in the organization we have risen. And no matter how much experience we have, we all have our limits and biases around approaching and understanding situations and challenges. By giving our team members opportunities to think through how to address our expectations themselves, we can see new and better opportunities in addressing the challenges or the deliverables that we have to deal with.

Another technique that is often helpful here with all three of the steps, is using a role and responsibility model that was actually developed by the U.S. Army well over ten years ago. Most of us would acknowledge that the U.S. Army manages some very large projects, sometimes called wars. The logistics of those projects are larger than many of us would ever experience.

Many years ago they came up with a role and responsibility model that they dubbed the RACI model. What they had learned was that most of the projects that went well had very clear roles and responsibilities for stakeholders in all functions, during every phase of the project.

How does this relate to creating conditions of accountability? It's part of setting clear and viable expectations, being clear about consequences, and a mechanism that we can use to hold ongoing conversations based upon facts.

I will quickly summarize the RACI model here. Basically, each one of the four letters stands for a role, and while the model is called RACI, I'm actually going to explain it as ARCI, because there is a hierarchy that maps to that sequence of the letters.

A is for Accountability. The Army determined that when no one is accountable, projects and initiatives tend to fail or at least have significant difficulty. Perhaps a little surprising is that when more than one entity or individual is accountable, there are similar difficulties in delivering results and holding people to task.

In the case of insufficient accountability, it's clear that without somebody being the place where the buck stops, decisions don't get made and directions are not set in a timely fashion. Less obvious, when there are multiple people or groups who believe they are accountable, finger pointing and abdication arise. One might say, "While I am accountable, I am not accountable for that part of it." Or there are people who believe that they share accountability but have difficulty establishing consensus.

Assuming that we have one party or function clearly accountable at any phase of a project process, then the next level down is Responsibility, R. There we have the individuals who are Responsible for actually doing the work or executing the tasks at that phase of the project.

Below that we have C, people who are in Consulting roles. These are people who may not necessarily have the responsibility of doing a significant amount of work, but they do have review and approval responsibility.

In the domain of information technology, it's not uncommon to also need review and approval by the legal department or compliance specialists. Certainly in other kinds of projects, there may need to be review and approval by departments that are not directly associated with the deliverable itself.

And finally, the I in the RACI model stands for Informed. This is the one level where there is no feedback loop. These are individuals or a function, who by agreement, need to be kept informed as to what is going on, but may not need to provide feedback in order for the process to continue.

In my management consulting, I have used this process to rescue and unstick projects that are in trouble. And, I have also used it to help launch projects that were successful. But for the purposes of Creating Conditions of Accountability, I believe it's enough to know about this RACI model. It's another tool that can be effectively used in executing the three-step process.

I'd like to move on to a couple of additional tools that can be used, particularly ways of identifying additional facts or empirical evidence in order to hold ongoing conversations.

One approach, particularly in projects, is to use what I

call a traffic light status reporting process. Basically, you identify all of the tasks that are part of a project or work plan. Based upon their status, code them either red, yellow, or green, and track the trend.

Obviously, you want more green than yellow or red. One simple way to work with empirical evidence is to track what I label the yellow trend. As long as from week to week yellow represents a smaller and smaller percentage of all of the tasks, green is getting larger, and red is non-existent (or at least not growing) then you have a positive trend. And that is one way to hold ongoing conversations based upon facts.

Another way to set clear and viable expectations, even before projects begin, is to use what we call the three constraint model. Whenever a request is made we often have three constraints that are interdependent.

One is the Scope of the request. Another is the budget available to us in delivering the on the scope of the request. And the third is the timeframe or delivery date.

As any experienced project or product manager knows, one or two of these can be specified as a requirement, but all three of them generally cannot because they are interdependent variables. It is certainly not unusual to have a request for a defined scope, with a set budget and a particular date, and to stand firm on those requirements.

To the extent that we can then introduce a model like this, to begin to quantify the impact of changing any one or two of the variables on the others, very often that will enable us to set clear and viable expectations and also hold conversations based upon empirical evidence.

Another area where I see a lot of leaders not leveraging all of the tools that are readily available, is to *empiricize* what I would call risk profiles. That's very simply plotting out the impact and the probability of any particular event or series of events, either in day-to-day operations or in the process of developing a product or delivering a project.

For instance, a low impact event with a low probability would wind up being a low risk situation to consider. A high impact, but very low probability incident might also be either a low or a medium sized risk to consider. However, it is possible to have a relatively low impact situation with a very high probability turning into a medium or high impact risk. As we go up the impact scale and the probability scale, we go from low risk to medium risk to high risk, to potentially catastrophic risk. And even a low probability incident, if the impact were high enough, could be viewed as a catastrophic risk. E.g., the complete physical loss of a data center could be catastrophic, when back up and recovery assumes less severe events like power outages.

It has been my experience in project management and product development, that very often our inability to quantify, or at least qualify, relative risks makes it difficult to create conditions of accountability and hold people to those conditions of accountability.

So far, in talking about creating conditions of accountability, it has been implied that we are creating conditions of accountability for people who report to us in our organizations. As most of us would acknowledge, that is probably not the most frequent situation in which we operate.

In fact, often we are called upon to manage up or across organizations. We all know the significant challenge when we don't have the positional power that we enjoy when we manage down into our own departments. Obviously, it's much easier to hold people accountable when we have positional power.

As I have often explored with coaching clients the importance of managing up, I find that relatively new managers don't realize the importance of managing up, or don't see it as the opportunity that it is. One reason that managing up has such high leverage for our leadership impact, and the reason that it's so important that we address it with this separate section, is that the higher one goes in an organization, the more impact that they tend to have, and the larger their capacity is to have impact.

When we effectively manage up, we are leveraging the potential impact that comes with the authority of those higher level positions, and not just the impact that comes directly from our own position. I remember one manager who had been in his role for about nine or ten months, and his approach to managing up was reporting what his team was doing. He did not see that managing up was also an opportunity to support his boss and people at even higher levels of the organization to become more effective in their roles and as leaders.

Back when I was working in a large organization and reporting to a C level executive, I would occasionally give him feedback on what was working and what was not working, so that he could choose if and where he wanted to change what he was doing. Periodically I also offered to take some of what was not working off of his plate, if it was something that he was less interested in doing. In that process, I was able to help him be more successful.

Much earlier in my career, I worked for a woman who was arguably brilliant at her core function, but her interper-

sonal skills scared a lot of the lower level people in the organization. At times, sales people would literally run for cover
when this merchandise buyer raised her voice and ranted and
raged. I suggested that she rant at me so, it would be clear that
it was me, and not them, that she was talking about so that they
wouldn't be frightened. That worked out very well, because I
certainly didn't take any of it personally. I understood that it
was just constructive feedback at a raised volume and a higher
pitch than normal conversation, and it enabled everyone to perform more effectively.

With that in mind as context for the importance of managing up, and some of the related challenges, here are some the
techniques. I often point out to my clients that managing up is
best done proactively. Before a senior leader has made a decision, it is far easier to influence the outcome of a their decision
process or assessment process, than to change it after a decision
has been made. To change a decision requires admitting that
that the earlier position had been a mistake.

Another mechanism is to articulate or create wins and
conditions of success. Sometimes when we seek to manage
up, there are expectations that are only about avoiding negative consequences, and we don't even know what a win would
look like. Again, in information technology, business leaders
very typically expect perfection 100% of the time and are unim-
pressed when anywhere near that level of service or reliability
is delivered.

One opportunity for leaders in IT organizations, is to
apply what we call the -1, 0, +1 Model. Where typically such
leaders would be seen as delivering only -1s or 0s, they can
actually reset expectations and collaboratively work with key

stakeholders to identify what we call the +1s, where outcomes can be identified that would be wins.

Again, this comes back to establishing or creating compelling consequences. If all of the consequences are negative, or the avoidance of negative consequences, we leave a very significant motivator (positive consequences) off the table.

Using the -1, 0, +1 Model to manage expectations and define them in such a way that there can be positive outcomes, provides us with another mechanism for creating conditions of accountability, especially when we are managing up rather than down into our organization.

Another mechanism that is popular with coaching clients is what we sometimes call the Upside-Down Snowman. Visualize a line drawing of a snowman made up of touching circles, but with the largest circle at the top. Then think of these as interlocking gears. The large circle or gear at the top represents senior level management, and then the smaller circles in the middle and the bottom represent people lower in the organizational hierarchy who are doing more and more of the work.

Typically someone high in the command chain gets an idea to have something done, and it appears to them to be relatively quick and simple. They make their request and their request goes down the hierarchy. With each layer down, think of these as interlocking gears that turn. The top-level executive gives his request to a senior vice president who sends his request to the group manager. The group manager looks at the request and assumes a team of three to four people can complete the task in a couple of days and passes the request to the department manager who assumes it will take four or five people two weeks to complete the task. At the bottom of the interlocking gears is the team that will do the work. They are the ones who realize it will take several months to complete the task, and then go ahead complete the project.

This often frustrates senior level leaders because if they had "known" how much work was ultimately going to be involved in what they thought was a relatively simple request; they would have never had the work done.

This illustrates how important it is to send feedback up the "snowman" chain, through the gears, and not assume that higher level management comprehends the amount of time involved in completing this work request. Lack of managing the expectations, and lack of holding ongoing conversations, based on evolving and emerging facts, sometimes prevent us from enabling accountability.

Feedback up the chain can be provided by saying, "We have designed the solution to your request, sir, and it looks like it is going to require six people and six months' of work. Is that in line with your expectations?" That creates a simple way to keep people accountable up the chain, as well as down the chain.

Another effective approach for managing up to create conditions of accountability is to use *The Power of a Positive No,* which we discussed in depth in Chapter 3. Just to recap, *The Power of a Positive No* is a way to say "no" to a specific request while saying "yes" while building and enhancing the relationship.

When we discussed being clear on intent and the importance of having a primary intention to continually enhance and build relationships, even when saying no is part of a transaction or a conversation, *The Power of a Positive No* is one tool to accomplish that. This demonstrates the use of the power of a positive no, again, in managing up to create conditions of accountability.

Earlier we discussed the interdependent variables of scope, date and budget. That can actually be even more effective when used as a tool in managing up, particularly when the requester takes a very strong position.

The risk assessment model can also be used, when managing up, to qualify or quantify risk associated with direction or decisions.

Part of creating conditions of accountability is the idea that we are helping people above us in the organization to more effectively hold themselves accountable for making better decisions.

And then, finally, another tool, that we call Portfolio Management. If you think in terms of managing an investment portfolio, where you want to have a balance of investment vehicles that are matched to your investment objectives, the same can be true for a series of tasks, collection of requests or projects or products that we manage. The mechanism can be fairly simple:

1. Clearly articulate the strategic business driver for the product or project in question.

2. Relate that strategic business driver to an operational business initiative.

3. Based upon the operational business initiative, tie in projects or products.

Then create what we would call the Portfolio, which is the matrix of the strategies, the initiatives, and the related projects.

As conversations occur around balancing workloads, allocating resources, and delivery dates, this becomes another tool based upon the facts or empirical evidence, in terms of the impact on the overall Portfolio.

To summarize, the series of tools and techniques to support the three-step process of creating conditions of accountability are:

1. Set clear and viable expectations.
2. Create compelling consequences, both positive and negative.
3. Hold ongoing conversations based upon the facts.

As I mentioned earlier, this also is the foundation for Performance Management and Professional Development, which we will now explore in the next chapter.

Chapter Seven
Performance Management and Professional Development
Or, "It's not enough to provide feedback, we also have to ensure behavior changes."

We are devoting a separate chapter to Performance Management and Professional Development, because all of the topics we've already covered, (Managing Strategic Intent, Prioritization & Time Management, Delegation, Creating Conditions of Accountability, as well as our next chapter on Communication) directly impact how we address and implement the practice of Performance Management and Professional Development.

In my coaching work, I am frequently asked to help clients deal with "difficult conversations." I learned many years ago that "difficult conversations" is the not-so-secret code for providing negative feedback in performance management situations. Over the years I've learned, through my own experience as well as the experience of hundreds of clients, that when approached effectively, performance management need not consist of difficult conversations.

This chapter is titled Performance Management and Professional Development because combining the two intentions in our mind, brings a more constructive approach to the discipline of enabling staff members to maximize their potential. This is a deliberately positive phrase to maximize potential.

Performance Management is not just about correcting mistakes. It has a much larger and higher purpose. When our intentions are clear we very likely experience better results and there is no need to have difficult conversations.

A recent coaching client, a relatively junior manager with a year of managerial experience, terminated a staff member who had been on a performance improvement plan. Though doing a bit better, the person wasn't meeting the necessary expectations. This was a first time the junior manager had presided over a termination situation. He was uncomfortable about it and we spent some time discussing the termination.

And at the beginning of the conversation, the focus was on what the junior manager had experienced, and how the terminated employee may have felt before, during, and after the termination. And after discussing that, I posed the question, "What was the impact of the situation on the rest of the team, over the many months that preceded and led up to the termination?"

My client looked at me, and for the first time in this conversation, he smiled and said, "I know the entire team is going to be better off as a result of this termination." Then he thought for a moment, his smile grew wider, and he said: "In fact, even though this happened a couple of hours ago, it's clear to me that the team is already better off. A weight has been lifted off of their shoulders. No one has said anything directly about this individual, who was at his desk this morning, disappeared without much conversation, and is now nowhere to be found. Everyone seems to know what has happened, even though no announcement has been made yet." As he thought about it some more, he said, "It's kind of interesting that there's already a palpable feel to the change of the environment in our work group."

That's another reason why Performance Management

and Professional Development is a separate chapter. Very often leaders don't pay enough attention to the impact of performance management on the entire team. Doing performance management effectively, with each and every member of the team, has a cumulative and overall impact on the entire team. We do not usually consider the direct impact on the rest of the team members, separate from their individual performance management conversations.

Any member of the team who is not holding his or her own has a negative impact on the reputation of the team, and on the tone and trust level within the team. Very often the rest of the team members need to step in and step up to address a lack of performance of an individual, because at the end of the day it does impact the entire team's reputation.

Further, the people we are leading are constantly assessing *our* performance as leaders. In their ongoing decision to be led by us, they are always looking at how effectively we deal with the domain of performance management. If we have the competence, skill, commitment, and courage to be proactive in the way that we approach this domain of expertise, we earn their respect and they are more likely to commit to follow and be led by us. To the degree that we shy away from or show any degree of hesitation or discomfort with managing performance, that has a negative impact on how we are perceived as leaders and, therefore, how effective we are as leaders.

With that in mind as the framing of Performance Management, let's dive into some of the specifics.

First is the question about timing in the practice of Performance Management. People that talk about "difficult conversations" often approach performance management as a periodic event that is often scheduled by their companies as a performance management and evaluation process. At the very least, most companies require semi-annual performance management conversations. One is usually at the end of the company's fiscal year as the formal written performance review, which is usually accompanied by the salary review process. Almost all companies also require an interim or a mid-term, somewhat less formal but still documented, performance review process where conversations are held between managers and all of their staff members. Some record is created as a result of those conversations.

In some companies that is the full extent of performance management, unless an unpleasant event transpires or somebody makes a significant mistake. Performance Management is often avoided until we absolutely, positively have to do it.

If you recall from the prior chapter on Creating Conditions of Accountability, the second step in that three-step process is to establish compelling consequences. We went into some depth about the need to have compelling positive consequences, as well as compelling negative consequences. By that definition, Performance Management needs to include conversations about positive results and outcomes, just as often, if not more often, than conversations about negative outcomes and situations.

Another reason that my clients perceive performance management conversations as somewhat difficult is that they are too infrequent. My experience has been that the more often I talk with staff members about their performance, the easier the conversations are. By virtue of making performance management conversations part of the everyday exchange, it tends to significantly de-emotionalize them. If we are continually talking about performance, and are effectively mixing positive feedback with what we euphemistically call constructive feedback, then there's very little reason for either leaders or team members to be concerned about the content of performance management conversations. And so, they cease to be difficult.

I invite you to think about a couple of different circumstances where something happened that wasn't quite right, and you had a conversation either immediately or shortly afterward with the employee. Now think of one or more times when in that situation, you had a fairly relaxed conversation stating that you knew they had been working hard but the deliverable wasn't quite what you expected

Contrast that with a situation where a team member missed several deadlines or delivered work products that were substandard in quality. Maybe the first few times you said to yourself that it was unusual, decided not to make a big deal of it so as not to upset the team member, and you waited and see what happened. Finally someone outside your organization, or a key stakeholder, pointed out to you that this team member's performance was substandard. At this point you couldn't wait to deal with this problem.

If you're like most of my clients, the situations that I've asked you to recall, should seem more than a little familiar. If so, I would hope that you can readily see that by having more frequent conversations about an individual's performance, and including the positive situations and calling them out for recognition, as well as the negative, all lead to less intense, less difficult, and more constructive performance management conversations. To the extent that those conversations are constructive and focus on performance improvement, they are important components of any professional development program or initiative. Very often we overlook the value that delegating stretch objectives to staff members can have in their professional development, as well as management of their performance.

I am sometimes asked by clients about letting people "fail." I have a very simple and strong position on that. My answer is, "No, it's never appropriate to let someone fail. But it is appropriate to allow someone to make mistakes." The art and the science of effective leadership in that domain is to effectively distinguish between mistakes and failure.

Obviously, smaller mistakes that are caught, identified and addressed in a timely fashion with corrective action do not cause failure. However, to the degree that mistakes are larger, or recognized later in any process, they have a larger impact until they cross that fine line which can lead to failure.

Most of us learn from our mistakes. Unfortunately, learning that occurs when we fail comes with a very undesirable side effect. Often that is loss of self-esteem, loss of confidence, a reduction in courage, and perhaps reduced trust for whomever put us in the situation where we failed.

There are many books on the market about how to gain trust, maintain trust, and how to build trust quickly. My experience is that trust is something that takes a very long time to build and something we are constantly building. Based on our actions, we build trust every moment of every day.

While it takes a long time to build a high level of trust with everyone with whom we interact, it is unfortunately very easy to lose that trust. Frequently, trust isn't lost a little bit at a time, but in big, huge, catastrophic chunks. Trust is hard to earn, easy to lose, and not something we want to mess with. So hence, another important reason for us to be very clear on how to approach effective Performance Management and Professional Development.

It would be beyond the scope of this book and this chapter to go into much more detail on how to manage the mistake/failure. If you have further questions, feel free to visit the "Ask Bob" page at our website, www.KantorConsultingGroup.com/AskBob/.

Now let's talk a bit about how we measure our effectiveness in performance management. Very often this is an area where people ask how to know if they're doing a good job. I often distinguish between metrics and measures in leadership development coaching work. There are few metrics when it comes to measuring the effectiveness of leadership, that can be directly tied back to leadership as the only contributing factor to those metrics. And I use the term "metric" as a behavior or result that can be quantitatively measured in a statistically significant fashion. If you're on a manufacturing line, it might be the number of defects. If you're an IT professional and you are coding and supporting applications, it might be the number of reported bugs. If you are an HR professional, it may be the number of interviewed candidates that actually get hired.

I often distinguish those kinds of "metrics" from "measures", where a measure is a qualitative and observable situation. Say we do 180-degree feedback programs and we take a look at the fact that some managers get much higher levels of positive feedback from their staff members than others. We may even categorize the feedback into various kinds of behavior. At the end of the day, that is still a qualitative measure because it depends upon an individual's opinion.

So, how do we know if we are doing a good job as performance managers? Ensuring that people aren't failing is certainly one viable measure. Secondly, we can look at the performance improvement of our organization or team in terms of measures of work performance. This is a measure because it is not entirely the result of performance management, but performance management certainly has an impact.

Is our reject rate going down? Is the number of widgets that we are producing during any production period going up? Are we doing customer satisfaction surveys where customer satisfaction is getting better? All of those could be measures that in some degree reflect how effectively we do performance management.

There's another measure that goes back over ten years to the publication of *First Break All the Rules,* by a couple of senior consultants from the Gallop organization, and often talked about in corporations today. One of the surprising conclusions in the book is that the quality of the relationship between an employee and their direct supervisor is what determines employee productivity and loyalty, much more so than pay, perks, benefits or workplace environment. This conclusion was based on a study of over 40,000 employees and determined that employees want supervisors that:

- Provide clear and consistent expectations,

- Treat them with respect,

- Value their unique qualities, and

- Encourage and support their growth and development.

All of those measures are, in fact, addressed by the six components of our Simple Leadership Life Cycle.

Those of us who do one-on-one meetings with our staff members as a way to elicit issues or concerns, all too often find that when we ask for that kind of feedback, we don't get answers. And, when we do get answers about issues, often those answers sound like people are complaining.

Instead of asking what issues or problems exist, I find it better to ask what would need to change in order for the work environment to be more positive, for productivity to increase, or for customer satisfaction to go up.

By focusing on and asking about what would need to change, we are requesting input, feedback and ideas for constructive changes. By focusing on actions that might make things better, we improve the context of the conversation and focus the discussion on positive outcomes that result in higher quality of feedback from our staff members. More importantly, staff members are more comfortable entering into the conversation because they no longer feel like they are raising problems without solutions and complaining. By contrast, they feel empowered and supported in thinking about how to solve problems, rather than just identify problems.

A further dimension of this approach is that in addition to engaging people more fully, it also creates a bias to action. When we ask what would have to change "so that...", or "in order to...", people are immediately thinking in terms of how action can contribute to such a change.

In talking with one very senior manager about this approach, he saw it as a wonderful way to problem solve without indicating blame or responsibility. In his particular case, one of his direct reports was not meeting his expectation in a particular domain of practice. He initially asked, "Your performance isn't measuring up, what do you need to do differently?" After our discussion, he changed his approach to, "What would have to change in order for your team to reduce its error rate from 20% to 5%?" And at that point, they were able to collaborate and co-create possibilities, including looking at some of the root causes for the relatively high rate of errors. They were also able to identify some larger issues that were a function of the environment, where the root causes went above and beyond this individual's department.

This senior manager began to use this same approach in skip level conversations where a lot of the more junior people in his organization were previously uncomfortable raising problems to him, believing that they were going around their managers. They became open to talking about what would need to change in order for improvements to be realized across the organization.

Coming back to the question of measurement and metrics for a moment, another way to look at the distinction between metrics and measures is to consider them as hard factors versus soft factors. Hard factors are those where we have hard data or statistics. The soft factors are those that are observable, but not quantifiable. Sometimes it is helpful for leaders to not only list all of the measures and metrics, or hard and soft factors, that they can identify, but to also then rank them in terms of which ones may correlate to desired outcomes.

When we see high degrees of correlation for soft factors, there are measures that can be further qualified or quantified to make them even more useful. For example: Say we do 180-degree feedback programs and we take a look at the fact that some managers get much higher levels of positive feedback from their staff members than others do. We may even categorize the feedback into various kinds of behavior.

And we might even quantify it a bit by saying that "X percent of your staff members said that you do a good job of sharing information with them" or "You do a good job of ensuring that they have the tools that they need to do their job." And at the end of the day that is still very much a qualitative measure because it depends upon an individual's opinion.

At the same time, by being able to provide a list of measures or metrics and weighting them, it gives us an opportunity to provide clear expectations to staff members about how we are going to measure performance against those expectations.

If you think back to creating conditions of accountability by setting clear and viable expectations, this is how we set the foundation for accountability. By being specific around measurement factors, we significantly enhance the foundation for accountability.

An example of performance management that I became aware of through one of my clients, is the idea of helping people learn how to simplify everything they do. A woman in middle management felt that, in spite of the fact that she had very strong and competent people, her organization wasn't delivering its full potential because everything "seemed too difficult and too complicated." She identified a goal to teach her staff to simplify, and that translated into performance management targets for all of them. And they identified targets for simplifying their approach to problem solving, designing solutions, managing projects, and interacting with clients. She got her staff excited about the potential that simplification would enable everyone on the team to realize huge leverage in their efficiency and overall effectiveness.

I believe that simplification is something that we, as leaders, don't often address with our teams. We tend to assume that everyone is already doing this, or that that it is a personality trait and not something that can be taught or learned. However, it absolutely can be taught and learned. It starts with realizing that simplification is a skill and technique that should be in play for everyone that we lead, including ourselves.

I would like to explore another action that each of us could take as leaders, to manage our own leadership performance and development by establishing a self-coaching plan.

Very often we approach performance management and professional development of our staff members with less rigor and structure than we do other important projects. Whether our role is product development, software development, customer service, or sales, more often than not, when we have a significant initiative, we create well structured, documented project plans, and routinely measure performance against those plans. Maybe the performance is reject rates, on-time delivery, or achievement of phases/stages of a deliverable or product development methodology. In any event, we use highly structured and fairly rigorous project or product management tools and techniques.

Too often I see that when it comes to professional development of ourselves and our team members, we take a much less rigorous and structured approach around professional development. We don't have the same level of plans to specify what is going to be achieved during the development period, and perhaps more importantly, to measure progress against those plans.

I recommend that as leaders we create project plans for development for ourselves as well as for all of our staff members. We should define the structure, the events, the outcomes, the milestones, the metrics, and then execute and track the progress.

A very simple structure for that is to create a matrix or spreadsheet, and list a handful of performance attributes as rows down the left column. It could be acquisition of a new skill, or improvement of soft skills, such as communication or project management. Then create columns across the top of matrix and label those columns Q1, Q2, Q3, and Q4, one for each quarter. For each quarter, we are seeking improvement in one or two activities, or one or two measures or metrics of success.

Review this with each staff member and/or have them develop the plan. By doing this you will have a document of shared understanding about the professional development targets. Then meet at least once a month to review progress against the plan. It is critical for success in this process to make sure that there are quarterly targets and monthly status meetings because at the end of month we can be confident that we are on track. This meeting and review process is something we should do with ourselves on our own plan, as well as with our staff members.

Using this approach, it is typical that no progress is made at the end of the first month, because professional development tasks often aren't a priority. So, at the end of the first month there are two more months in the quarter to get back on track and to make progress. This can be reviewed monthly to be certain progress is being made.

If progress is limited, I encourage people to not only commit to getting back on track, but to also take a look at what needs to change and/or what is getting in the way of doing an effective job of staying on track with professional development objectives.

And then at the end of the quarter, hopefully the professional development objective has been met. Certainly it's possible that in any one quarter, any one of the objectives may be behind schedule. This is an opportunity to do trend assessment.

If, however, more than one of the objectives is late in any quarter, or if all of the objectives tend to be running late, take a step back and to reassess what needs to change in order for your or their performance management and professional development practices to be more effective.

With that, let's move on to the chapter on Communication, the foundation for all of the other practices.

Chapter Eight
Communication
Or, "It's not enough to be clear, we also need to be understood."

The sixth of the leadership processes that make up the Simple Leadership Life Cycle is communication. We save it for last in the leadership development coaching process because it is the core foundation for everything that we do.

I don't mean to minimize the importance of the other five. Obviously, we wouldn't have a complete cycle if didn't have all of the components:

- Managing Strategic Intent;

- Prioritization and Time Management;

- Delegation;

- Creating Conditions of Accountability;

- Performance Management and Professional Development; and

- Communication.

Over the years, we have boiled down our approach to leadership to just those six, because we believe that they are the minimum number of core attributes that are required for effective leadership.

That brings me to a discussion about what we mean when we use the word "communication." Here is one of our favorite quotes:

"We cannot not communicate.

We are always and constantly communicating.

However, we may not always be communicating

or creating the results that we intend to create."

Paul Watzlawick

Very often in our coaching, when we do an assessment about strengths and development opportunities, clients tell us that they are very good communicators. I always inquire as to what evidence they consider when they make that assessment. This is a coaching technique to seek additional clarity on any assessment or any assertion by understanding what evidence or data points people are reflecting on when they make assertions or reach conclusions.

When I ask how they know they're a good communicator, clients frequently say that they get feedback that they articulate their positions well, they know they structure arguments well, or they know that they state things clearly. Yet, when we look at some of the leadership challenges that they have, we often hear that they "sent a clear message," or staff "knew what they had to do," or they were "told several times."

Clearly there is more to the equation than sending the message. And that, in fact, is the crux of our belief, position and practice around communication. Communication is not what we say, and not the message we deliver; it's the outcome that we create. Another way think about it is that it's not the message we send, it's the meaning that is received. Effective communication requires active engagement as a result of having and growing a relationship with the people with whom we communicate.

It the prior chapters, we've touched upon several important elements for establishing, building, and evolving a relationship. This includes a clear intention, effectively delegating, creating conditions of accountability, etc. So here, we'll just focus on the mechanism, or model, for leveraging the relationships that are built with those practices, as well as what it means to actively engage people.

Communication includes sending the message and ensuring that the action or result that we are after is agreed upon. This topic is covered very nicely in a book that is part of the original *One Minute Manager* series by Ken Blanchard and his associates. If you haven't read the title in this series called *The One Minute Manager Meets the Monkey*, it's a wonderful model for supporting the practice of effective communication and everything else that we've been talking about in the book.

There is an effective communication life cycle that is very much like a project life cycle or development life cycle, where you reverse the active listening process. In active listening, we frequently repeat to people what we believe we are hearing from them, and then we inquire as to whether we are accurately understanding what they are saying.

When we reverse active listening as part of our effective communication life cycle, we ask people what they believe, based upon what they are hearing from us, and ask them what they plan to do as a result of our conversation.

Very often in coaching, our clients say that after they've had a conversation with one of their team members, they test clarity with a question like, "Was I clear?" or "Do you understand?" Invariably, the answer is, "Yes, you are clear," or "Yes, I understand." Unfortunately, in far too many cases, there isn't enough active listening in that simple conversation to ensure that either or both parties correctly assesses the meaning in a mutual way. It is much better to ask what they plan to do or make happen as a result of the conversation. By doing this we can get a much stronger sense of how our message was received and what meaning our colleague took from our conversation.

Several years ago I worked with an applications development group that was having difficulty convincing a business management team to support an investment to replace an aging human resources system. The application team was asserting that because the older application was no longer being supported by the vendor, that the firm's ability to continue operating was at significant risk. The management team heard the argument and declined to support or approve the investment of over $1 million to replace the aging system.

Time went by. The application group came back to the management team, made a similar argument, and the management team again respectfully declined. After several iterations of this, we sat down with one of the senior members of the management team and asked a very simple question, "Do you believe that the business would cease to operate if the old HR system stopped running?" We learned that the senior executive actually believed that if the old HR system stopped running, the company could manage things manually until such time that the old system was repaired. That belief was a complete surprise to the applications professionals, because their belief was it was not possible to manually cover the processes that had been automated by the old system long ago. They had many good reasons for why:

1. The people who might have understood and known the processes to do that manually were no longer with the company. They had been replaced or assigned

elsewhere.

2. The policies and procedures that had been in place before the system had been installed 10 years ago were long out of date.

3. With all of the automation that had occurred, it was no longer possible to do things manually and then get the manually generated information back into the automated system, if and when the system was fixed and running again.

In further conversations we discovered yet another significant difference in belief. It turned out that the senior manager from the management team also believed that by virtue of the fact that this old system had run for so long without major incidents, that was a good indicator that there was nothing to worry about, and because it was so stable that it would continue running for a long period of time.

In fact, the applications team believed that just the opposite was the case; that because this system was so old, and much of the technology environment had evolved while this old application had not, that the system was becoming less stable, and therefore the likelihood of a catastrophic failure was growing with each passing year.

When each of the parties made their beliefs more visible and clear to the other, real communication finally occurred. It didn't take long before the management team reversed their earlier decision and readily approved the investment of over $1 million to replace the aging system.

You'll notice that as I recounted that story, I used the term "believe" many times. I'd like to share now a very simple and fundamental communication model that is not typically used in the business environment.

Very often when we think about communication, we focus on the message that we are sending, which means that we are focusing on the information that we need to share, and we call that "focusing on what people need to know." Often we think that by simply sending a message and sharing a set of information, that we have communicated. And, the clarity of what we send to people determines the effectiveness of our communication.

We prescribe a simple three-step process for communication, and every one of the steps is critical to communicate effectively:

1. Focus on what people need to know.

2. Understand what people believe.

3. Be clear about what we want people to do.

I'd like to credit my colleagues, Gregg Baron and Jeff Grimshaw, with this model that I have applied hundreds of times in my own work. And, my clients have applied it many more times in their work, and it has withstood the test of time.

One change that I have made over the years when applying the model is to use a reverse engineering approach, so that the first step is to articulate what it is we want people to do as a result of our communication. Do we want them to:

- Change their behavior?

- Change a decision?

- Make a decision along a particular path? or

- Support someone else in changing a behavior or

making a decision?

Often when I work with a client around improving their ability to obtain results based upon improving communication, we find that lack of sufficient clarity around the desired outcome is part of the challenge. Once we're clear about what we want people to do, then the critical missing step is to be very clear about what people currently believe, and what they need to believe in order to do what we want them to do. We can then determine what, if any, gap exists. It's the belief that they need to have, or the gap that exists, that determines what they need to know and what we need to focus on with our messaging in order to have effective communication.

All too often when we try to answer the "what do we need to communicate" question, we are so focused on our own beliefs and perspective that we assume that sharing the information that is important to us is communicating effectively. Sometimes that is the case, but many times that results in insufficient and ineffective communication.

We call the model Know, Believe and Do. We suggest reversing the sequence:

1. Be clear about what it is that we want people to do.

2. Clarify what they need to believe in order to do that by understanding what they believe today.

3. Identifying the gap, and then putting our messaging together to be able to address that gap.

Very often clients ask how to find out what people believe. That frequently points us to yet another step in the communication process. Sometimes we need to spend time doing research into what they believe, why they believe it, or on what evidence they are currently basing those beliefs.

Sometimes, even when we know what we want people to do or what decision we want them to support, we need to spend time with them asking them questions and using the active listening process to get very clear on their beliefs. It may be that in the moment of discovering that information, it's premature to try to communicate and change those beliefs.

Depending upon how large the gap is, we may need to focus only on understanding their current beliefs, and then allow ourselves more time, (hours, days or weeks) to reassess and construct a message or do additional research and fact gathering to support the messaging.

Sometimes when I talk with clients about this process, I call it pragmatic communications. Stephen Covey in his original book, *The 7 Habits of Highly Effective People*, talked about this very simply when he said, "Begin with the end in mind." I throw that out as another part of the foundation in terms of being clear on what we want people to do before reverse engineering the messaging itself.

Implementing this model is fairly simple, although as we've discussed in some of the other leadership attributes, it's not always easy. Quite often when I work with clients in a technical discipline, like information technology, engineering, chemistry or biology, we discover that too often when they communicate with people outside of their area of expertise, they over-communicate with way too much detail.

I worked with one middle manager who had gotten quite a bit of feedback from his manager and his business sponsors, that he was difficult to understand. In his very first coaching session with him, as I was listening to him go on and on, it became very clear that part of his problem was he didn't know when to stop communicating. So we talked about that at length and came up with a very simple filter for him. We called it The 90 Second Rule.

He began to pay attention to time when he was talking and tried to stop himself, at least once every 90 seconds, to assess how his message was being received and/or to invite feedback or comments from whomever he was talking with. As he got better at this practice, he refined the process so that he could stop and use body language to create an opening for the other individual to engage in the conversation with him. Over time he became more and more nuanced in the practice.

Another model that we invite people to apply is the age-old Newspaper Pyramid. For those of you who still read newspapers, or can remember reading a newspaper, the entire news story is frequently contained in one phrase called the "headline," and if the headline peaks your interest, then you read further. What you may not be aware of is that the traditional newspaper story pyramid chunks stories into three sections and goes into further and further detail on a repeating basis.

After the headline, the first three paragraphs that follow the headline give you a very high-level synopsis of the story. If you read just the first three paragraphs, you technically know the entire story but without very much detail. If after reading that far you want to know more about the story, then as you read the next three paragraphs, you get the same story but at a finer level of detail. And if after reading those three paragraphs you have enough of the detail, then you can move on to another story, confident that you haven't missed any important aspect.

If, on the other hand, you're still interested or find the story useful, you can read the next three paragraphs and get yet another layer of detail, and so on, until you actually reach the end of the story.

We coach our clients to use the very same pyramid style and to tell the entire story at a very high level as quickly as possible, and then to interact using active listening with their colleague to determine whether or not there's a shared understanding around the communication, and whether there has been enough of a connection for the individual to do what they want them to do, or whether another layer of detail is appropriate.

That basically sums up the mechanism for effective communication. It obviously relies a great deal on the other five attributes that we've already covered in detail earlier chapters. There are thousands of books written about the subject of communication, and we all understand that attitude, tone, body language, and many other subtle attributes play into the effectiveness of communication as well.

As the focus of our book is the Simple Leadership Life Cycle, we have sought to keep every one of the six components very basic, so that everyone can come up to speed quickly and perfect the processes as quickly and easily as possible.

We end the chapter on communication at this point and will close the book by delving into the implementation of these processes, with more specific examples and several subthemes that further flesh out what we've covered in the foundational six processes.

Chapter Nine
Making It Happen
Or, "It's not enough to know, we also need to act."

That concludes the discussion on how to implement the Simple Leadership Life Cycle in order to build the core and critical skill set that we described as Leadership in the first chapter.

We suggest that in today's complex, socially networked world, that Leadership is a core competency for each and every one of us, whether manager, individual, contributor, parent, child, volunteer, community member, or committee member. We could each be more effective if we strengthened the core leadership behaviors that make up the Simple Leadership Life Cycle.

Having discussed all six of them, hopefully in enough depth that you feel comfortable putting them into practice, this last chapter is focused on how you can take what you now know and put it to use, thereby changing the way you behave in multiple situations on a day-to-day basis. This chapter will discuss how to habitualize these best leadership practices. As with the practices themselves, our approach is very simple.

The **first step** is to write down each of the six behaviors or attributes with a very brief description of each. Next, list the three-step model to support them.

The **second step** is to use that list of the six behaviors and to check your performance at the end of each day. In other words, as you're wrapping up for whatever your day turns out to be, take a look at the list, and simply ask yourself, "Did I apply each and every one of those today?" Your first thought may be that you won't have an opportunity to apply each and every one of them every single day. I would suggest that you probably do or will have that opportunity.

Again, if you go back to Chapter Two where we discussed the Simple Leadership Life Cycle and why we created the model to be a cycle, the premise was that we apply all of those activities all day long, across multiple situations and opportunities. And we even cycle through them over and over again in dealing with some of the more complex situations and opportunities that we face.

I would assert that most of us, during the course of just living our lives, can and should leverage each one of these six behaviors every day for the better part of the day.

Coming back to the list, make sure that you can identify that you are applying these practices. You may simply want to look at the list and ask yourself:

- "Was there a point in the day where I set my Intention?
- Did I begin my day with Prioritization?
- Did I check on where I was against my Priorities several times during the day?"
- "Did I have my eye out for opportunities to Delegate work that I didn't get to, or that wasn't appropriate for me?
- Did I do an effective job of Delegating?"
- "In the process of Delegating, did I create Conditions of Accountability using the structure that I've learned as part of this process?

- Did I take checkpoints during the day with several different individuals to do Performance Management and Professional Development? And, did I do that effectively?"

- Did I Communicate with anyone today? And if so, how effective was my approach to that Communication?"

We should be applying all of these activities each and every day. Was there a day in the last couple of months where you didn't communicate? The idea is to go through the list and ensure that you are applying them, and take that quick checkpoint as to whether you are doing them effectively. You cannot improve performance if you are not first aware of the behavior or the lack of the behavior. Next, determine whether the behavior is as strong as you want it to be.

The **third step** in this process, is to identify one or two instances during the day when you either did apply the behavior or should have applied the behavior, but want greater improvement. Spend a couple of minutes thinking about how you might have applied the behavior differently, and use that as a learning opportunity and reference point to carry forward into the next couple of days.

You might choose to write some of that down, but I generally find that's not necessary. Simply bringing your awareness to the situation and focusing on it for a couple of minutes can have a huge positive impact on your practice of leadership, if you do it consistently each day for at least a month.

Remember, 30 days is the magic number for habitualizing significant behavior changes. This is supported by the NASA astronauts where the prism glasses inverted their field of vision by 180 degrees but their visual fields flipped back to "normal" in 30 days

That's why the **first step** of this process of becoming a much stronger leader is to measure your performance on each of these six dimensions. The **second step** is to strive to improve for at least 30 days. The **third step** is to periodically ask the people around you for feedback. Whether or not you ask for feedback, people will be talking about what you're doing and how you are doing it. So if you don't ask for feedback, you may be the only one who doesn't know how you're doing, because anyone who is critical will be sure to tell other people what they know.

There are a couple of simple approaches for requesting feedback. Focus on one of the behaviors and in casual conversation simply ask someone, whose opinion you value, how are you doing. Along with setting your intent, it can be even more powerful if you build trust and set the stage by first explaining that you have been working on improving your skills. If you are making the kind of progress you believe you are, there should be observable changes and improvements. Therefore, take a moment to ask if they have observed any instances where you're doing a better job.

Hopefully you'll get good news, and every now and then you won't. The bottom line is that if you're not measuring and not testing, then you won't have the information that you need to actually make improvements.

Another approach, a little less specific to the steps in the Simple Leadership Life Cycle, is to hold what I call a Simple 180-Degree Feedback conversation . It's 180 versus 360, because generally you go laterally across the organization and down, although you can do it as a 360 and go up, as well. As with our other processes, there are three steps, or one step with three questions.

We suggest that you identify the handful of individuals from whom you want feedback and send them an email message. Explain that you are doing an informal feedback initiative and are reaching out to a handful of people whose opinions you value. Request a 10-minute meeting to hear their feedback on three questions. Then present to them, in the email message, these three questions:

- "What am I doing that I should keep doing?"
- "What am I not doing that I should start doing?"
- "What am I doing that I should stop doing?"

At the end of the message, ask them to come up with just one or two brief answers for each of the three questions, and be prepared to share their thoughts during the 10-minute meeting you will schedule as a follow-up.

A couple of points about the specifics of the request:

1. We highly advise you to make the email request ahead of the meeting so the person you are asking for feedback has sufficient time to reflect. When you ask someone in the moment, the quality of the feedback is often not nearly as high as if they've had a couple of hours or a few days to give it some thought.

2. By asking ahead of time, you're not putting the individual on the spot when you sit down at the meeting. Sometimes when we ask people for what may be critical feedback, they may react with discomfort to being in that situation.

3. Make your intention for holding the follow up meeting perfectly clear, by providing the detail after the comment or request for feedback.

4. Specifically request that their feedback be given in the meeting conversation, rather than via an email response, because that gives us a couple of opportunities to:

   a. Ask clarifying questions in the moment, and

   b. Deepen our relationship by having another point of contact face-to-face in real time.

Over the years we've seen that sometimes feedback is not specific enough for us to understand how to action it. Hopefully the questions are designed to elicit behavioral feedback, so that that won't be an issue. By having the conversation face-to-face you can ask for examples to better understand their feedback.

Another approach to help habitualize and improve these behaviors is to use another awareness tool we call Listening for Difficulty. Any time we find ourselves in "the zone", the work that we're doing and the situations we're in seem easy and effortless. If you recall the model of Conscious Competence, we are Unconsciously Competent when we are working in the zone, where everything seems to be easy and we appear to be operating in a state of grace.

When I work with coaching clients, I often invite them to become more aware of when a situation feels difficult or uncomfortable. Rather than simply struggling against the difficulty or being uncomfortable, I urge them to take a step back and to ask,

"Why is it hard? What are my issues here, or opportunities to lead and perform better?" Following this question will be realizations such as:

- "I'm struggling in this conversation is because I'm not clear on my intention."
- "I'm feeling overwhelmed right now because I haven't spent time prioritizing. "
- "I'm not clear about my priorities."
- "I've got too much on my plate right now is because I haven't been delegating."
- "I don't have someone with enough skill to delegate to [Catch 22] because I haven't been proactively delegating as a way to develop my talent."
- "I'm not getting the results I want with business partners and staff because I haven't done an effective enough job creating conditions of accountability."
- "The reason I am surprised that this project is not complete is because I did not do an effective job of setting up and maintaining conditions of accountability."

To the extent that we can be aware of when things are difficult or hard for us, we can point to opportunities to improve what we are doing and better habitualize and implement these leadership practices.

Many years ago, one of my coaches helped me become aware of what I was doing well and what needed improvement. He suggested that weaknesses are often strengths that we overuse. That was quite an "Aha" for me, because one of my key strengths had been the ability to analyze and to manage detail.

In the prior several months, I had taken on some new responsibilities that required that I not get absorbed by detail and not focus on analysis. The skills that had gotten me to that point were no longer sufficient to carry me forward; I had to begin using additional strengths and skills.

One way that I sometimes discuss this with clients is the idea of survival of the fittest as an evolutionary driver. When Darwin made the assertion that the fittest survive, he did not mean to suggest that it was the strongest who survived. In several of his essays, Darwin made it clear that it was the most flexible, agile, and adaptable organisms that survived, because they were, in fact, the fittest. So, context becomes a key for us.

We've talked in this chapter about raising our awareness and becoming more sensitive to when things are difficult, when things are working, when they're not working, and when getting more feedback would be helpful. A critical success factor to being flexible, agile and more effective, is to better understand the context within which we are operating and look at how to improve our application of the six core Leadership skills.

The program that we have laid out with the Simple Leadership Life Cycle is a combination of very simple techniques. There are no complex models or processes. Most of the techniques have three simple steps, are easy to remember and simple to do. As we discovered with the clasping of hands exercise at the beginning of the book, even the simplest of behavior changes are not always easy to integrate into our regular routines. This is where practice and repetition come into play.

Again, it took 30 days for the visual field of the NASA astronauts to flip, and it takes time and effort applying these behaviors. There will be a period where they are uncomfortable, until we get to the point where they are ours to apply with unconscious competence.

It is not uncommon when we first try some of these techniques, to see our performance actually go down, because new behaviors are often not as well executed as old behaviors are, even though they are ultimately more effective. I invite you to apply one of these new skills and to stick with it for at least several days or weeks until you see a positive change in your results and outcomes.

This is where coaching can become a useful or critical success factor, and can become a differentiator between success and failure as sustainable improvement in your leadership skills. If any of these skills or behaviors continue to frustrate you, look into finding someone either inside or outside your organization who can mentor or coach you to more effectively apply them.

Another distinction about our approach to the Simple Leadership Life Cycle and its components, is that we leverage what we call Project Planning and Management Skills. In fact, more than half of our coaching practice is with Information Technology managers, most of whom have strong project management skills and are accustomed to applying them to project initiatives. That is a very useful skill when applied to their own leadership development that can yield significant benefits. When we bring our IT leadership framework into the conversation and they explore the elements or tasks within our framework, they begin to put tasks and measures in place and evolve their IT Leadership Development Project Plan.

We discussed that in Chapter 7 as a Self-Coaching Plan, to tie together the concepts of checking how we're doing, seeking feedback from somebody who can mentor or coach us, and having a plan in place from which we can operate. Whether we call it a Self-Coaching Plan or a Leadership Development Project Plan, the key to success is to sit down periodically, at least once a month, to review our actual performance against our quarterly milestones.

This would probably be a useful place to share another observation around how we are wired and how we behave, particularly as it relates to assessing our performance and contrasting that to how we assess the performance of others. More often than not, when we assess the performance of other people, we look at what they do. We look at their behavior and compare it against the benchmarks of our expectations. And when their behaviors match, they are meeting our expectations. When they are better, they are exceeding our expectations. And, when they don't measure up, then they are not meeting our expectations.

We have observed over the years that most of us assess our own behavior or our own performance, not on our behavior, but on our intentions. If we intended to communicate more effectively by beginning with clarifying the outcome we were expecting and analyzing what beliefs our target audience held, then we are likely to assess that we had improved our practice of communication. In fact, we may not have not actually been doing that. Because often, we don't recognize that our behavior has not reflected our intention.

I frequently see this in my coaching work. When I sit down with clients and ask them how things are going related to any one of the practice improvement areas, they almost always say it's going well. But what they're telling me about turns out to be their intention.

When I acknowledge their assessment and ask them

for the evidence upon which they are basing their assessment, sometimes there's excellent evidence because they truly are making wonderful progress. And, sometimes there really isn't any evidence, or the evidence is contradictory, and that's where the coaching process can be very helpful.

I encourage everyone to routinely sit down and look at what their target was for the quarter, or for that point in their Project Plan for Leadership Development, and to get very clear on what behavior they have demonstrated or others have observed. By doing this you can accurately assess if you are making the progress you are striving to make.

Finally, I think it may be helpful to have a brief conversation about the difference between training, mentoring and coaching, as it relates to developing knowledge and skills. There are many excellent training programs and books on leadership skill development. When we take a training program in any of these leadership skills, our knowledge certainly improves.

In the training course itself, if we do role-playing, we can observe our skill improving. And very often when we first come out of such a training program and go back to into our work environments, that heightened level of skill remains with us for a couple of days, and sometimes for a couple of weeks.

Unfortunately, it is typical that the skill practice degrades and goes back almost to the level it was before the training occurred. While there's almost always some positive residual effect, bringing the new skill back to our real world often frustrates and challenges us to apply a very structured set of principles or processes, in an environment that was not addressed by the training program.

That's why having access to a coach or mentor as we

strive to apply the new skills can help us:

- Be accountable to ensure that we continue to apply what we've learned; and

- Work through how to adapt and adjust the knowledge that we have learned so we can continue to build the skills.

When we try to apply those new skills in the real world, as opposed to role play in the classroom, we find that our real time application of those still underdeveloped skills leaves us with a disappointing level of performance. This results in frustration, perhaps even embarrassment, so we let it go and decide to never try again.

Neil Rackham of Huthwaite Incorporated, a national sales training firm, and author of *SPIN Selling*, did a study with Xerox Corporation. In the study they looked at classroom-based training and followed up for months to see to what degree the newly acquired skills remained in place. They determined that about 87% of the new skills that were learned in a classroom environment were lost within several months after returning to the routine work environment, unless they were regularly reinforced with some kind of a coaching program. That translated into $0.87 on each skills training dollar being lost. We believe that is not atypical for much of the skills-based training that corporate America invests in today.

With that in mind, we urge you to practice and to hold yourself accountable for improving your observable behavior. Do it for at least 30 days, preferably for an entire year, so that you can instantiate the skills and behavioral improvements that we have discussed in this book.

We encourage you to stay in touch with us via our website, www.KantorConsultingGroup.com. Look there for updates to the material in this book. Use the "Contact Us" capabilities on the "Ask Bob" tab for follow-up questions and problems that you may have.

Chapter Ten
Start Right Now
Or, "We judge others by their behaviors, but we judge ourselves by our good intentions."

As we bring this book to a close, having gone through the six practice areas that comprise the Simple Leadership Life Cycle, it is apparent that there is overlap among each one of the six practices. This is one of the reasons that we illustrate the six practices as part of a continuous cycle.

On any one day, it is likely that we as leaders are practicing every one of the six components at different times during the day, on different projects, with different members of our team or key stakeholders.

As we move through the four stages of skills development we covered in the Delegation chapter, (moving from unconscious incompetence, to consciously incompetent, to consciously competent, and finally to unconsciously competent) the distinctions between the six Life Cycle compnents begin to disappear. Setting our intent is as much a part of prioritizing and managing our time as it is part of what we delegate and how we choose to delegate. Creating conditions of accountability are integrated with delegation and prioritization, as well as performance management.

Every one of the first five practices has a very strong component of communication, and relies heavily upon effective communication for the practice to have the impact that we expect and desire.

At the end of the day, drawing the lines between the six components of the Simple Leadership Life Cycle is a bit arbitrary. At the same time, there has been some degree of repetition between chapters. Our intent was to:

1. Show the integration of all of the pieces; and

2. Reinforce as we went, especially since some readers will skip around and may start with the material meets their most immediate need.

Therefore, it is important that each chapter could stand alone and deliver value on its own merits, and would include a bit of the overlapping material in the appropriate chapters.

The final step to derive real value from this book, is to make a decision to change our behavior and pick a place to begin. It's very easy, looking at all of the potential change that we could adopt, adapt and integrate into our leadership practices, to feel overwhelmed by the task. If you don't mind the cliché, "Each journey begins with one step." Please, pick the one that you feel will either give you the most leverage or be the most comfortable, or with which you will be most likely to succeed.

Whatever it takes to begin the journey, or to continue the journey if you are already well along the path, please, simply take the next step, practice or apply what appeals to you in the book, and let me know how it goes.

Visit our website for ongoing updates via our Notes on Leadership and blog entries. If you haven't already done so, please register for that so you can receive continuing updates to this material.

Visit the cio.com website and search for articles written by "Bob Kantor", to find more examples of this and related material.

Also, please feel free to use the "Ask Bob" page on our website to pose whatever questions you have, either now as a result of reading the book, or at any time in the future when applying some of the tools, techniques or ideas, if something isn't working quite right for you. We will do our best to answer your questions and give you support so that you, too, can realize the same success as our coaching clients.

I hope that you derive as much benefit and enjoyment from applying this material, as we have in creating it over the course of several years, and in working it with hundreds of clients.

Thank you for your time and interest.

About the Author

Bob Kantor has held a variety of leadership roles in IT and consulting, as both a business strategist and senior technology leader. He currently is the Principal of Kantor Consulting Group and is an accomplished author, speaker, coach and consultant.

Bob has been delivering leadership coaching to more than 100 IT managers in a culturally diverse global financial services company for the past two years, as well as to members of the CIO Executive Council.

Kantor has been providing leadership coaching and IT management consulting in a wide range of industries since the early 1990s. Functional specialties include IT, engineering and product development. Clients range from a $7B global financial services company to a $6M software firm.

In addition to his coaching and consulting roles, he is a co-author of the book, *No Winner Ever Got There Without a Coach*, and regular article contributor to cio.com. Bob is also an accomplished public speaker and a weekly guest on radio station VOCM's Morning Show, discussing leadership, management and career topics.

Kantor's experience spans several top industry leaders, including holding roles as Executive Director, IT Management Services for KPMG, Director of R&D Programs at Lotus Institute for Lotus Development Corporation, CIO for US Homecare Corporation, and Internal IT Consultant for Ciba-Geigy Corporation.

Bob lives with his wife Kathy and dog Zeus in the lower Hudson Valley in New York State, and enjoys hiking, photography, and watercolor painting.

To learn more about how you can engage Bob to enhance leadership and organizational effectiveness at your company, please go to www.KantorConsultingGroup.com.